Battlespace 1865

To Pete Peters who shared his appreciation of the Platte Valley and his knowledge of the people, history and subtleties of the region. We could not have done this project without Pete's involvement and would not have wanted to.

Battlespace 1865

Archaeology of the Landscapes, Strategies, and Tactics of the North Platte Campaign, Nebraska

by

Douglas D. Scott, Peter Bleed and Amanda Renner

AMERICAN LANDSCAPES

American Landscapes is an imprint of Oxbow Books

Published in the United Kingdom in 2016 by
OXBOW BOOKS
The Old Music Hall, 106–108 Cowley Road, Oxford OX4 1JE

and in the United States by
OXBOW BOOKS
1950 Lawrence Road, Havertown, PA 19083

Paperback Edition: ISBN 978-1-78570-339-3
Digital Edition: ISBN 978-1-78570-340-9

A CIP record for this book is available from the British Library

Library of Congress Control Number: 2016950100

Printed and bound in the United States of America
Typeset in the UK by Frabjous Books

For a complete list of titles, please contact:

UNITED KINGDOM
Oxbow Books
Telephone (01865) 241249
Fax (01865) 794449
Email: oxbow@oxbowbooks.com
www.oxbowbooks.com

UNITED STATES OF AMERICA
Oxbow Books
Telephone (800) 791-9354
Fax (610) 853-9146
Email: queries@casemateacademic.com
www.casemateacademic.com/oxbow

Oxbow Books is part of the Casemate Group

Front cover: Fort Mitchell as recalled from about the time of the Civil War, watercolor by W. H. Jackson *c.* 1933 (courtesy Nebraska State Historical Society)

Back cover, left to right: A Cheyenne biopictographic depiction of warriors attacking soldiers (courtesy History Colorado, Cheyenne Sketchbook 10036210); 12-pdr Mountain Howitzer; Courthouse and Jail Rocks (courtesy of National Park Authority, Scotts Bluff National Park); a mounted soldier of the 11th Ohio Volunteer Cavalry (courtesy Wyoming State Archives, Bretney Collection, 25810)

Contents

Acknowledgements

A great many people have aided our research efforts in developing the Battlespace concepts and theory. We are grateful to everyone. We wish to particularly thank and acknowledge the students of the 2008 and 2009 University of Nebraska Department of Anthropology archaeological field schools who did the yeoman work of metal detecting and recording the artifacts found at Rush Creek. The initial field work at Mud Springs involved Dr Melissa Connor, Colorado Mesa University, Professors Jerry Renaud and Luis Peon-Casanova of the UNL Broadcast program, and William Altizer, Ben Barnette, Penny Berger, John Feltz, Katherine Lamie, James Lindsay, Pete Peters, and Brian Schilz. The project was supported by a grant from the University of Nebraska-Lincoln, Vice Chancellor for Research.

Lt Col. John Blankenhorn and Lt Col. Lee Bokma of the University of Nebraska-Lincoln ROTC program introduced us to the battlespace model and FM-3 Operations manual. We are grateful for their help in developing our ideas. Major Nathan Ledbetter provided many insightful comments and during a number of conversations helped us better understand the intent and nature of FM-3. We also grateful to our archaeological colleagues, Dr Glenn Foard, University of Huddersfield, UK; Drs Tony Pollard and Iain Banks of the University of Glasgow, Scotland; Dr Steven Smith, Institute of Archaeology and Anthropology, Columbia, SC; and Charles Haecker, US National Park Service, Santa Fe, NM who engaged us in many thoughtful discussions about battlespace in a variety of contexts over the last several years. Kristen McMasters, American Battlefield Protection Program, National Park Service, deserves a special thank you for her willingness to allow us to develop some of the ideas presented here as part of a grant to UNL to develop a multiple property context for the Platte River valley during the Civil War. Her valuable insights and those of the other reviewers of the context document helped us build an initial operational model of what we now title battlespace.

Jim Potter as well as the staff of the Nebraska State Historical Society research room pointed us to many sources. The University of Nebraska Interlibrary loan staff did yeoman work in finding many an obscure reference during our research.

Steve Haack of Lincoln, Nebraska shared his research in the Bent-Hyde archives. He also graciously shared his deep knowledge of Nebraska and eastern Wyoming history. We cannot thank him enough.

Conrad Fisher and Ed Whitedirt of the Northern Cheyenne Tribe visited the Rush Creek battlefield while fieldwork was in progress and discussed both the discoveries and their significance. We sincerely appreciate their interest and the effort that was involved in their visit.

Battlefields of the 1865 North Platte Campaign happen to be owned and managed by private land owners. The Cape family has understood the importance of the Mud Springs Station for three generations. Rick Newkirk knew about the fighting of 1865 and, with careful management, preserved the terrain where we found the battle debris. These people welcomed our interests and tolerated our intrusions. Bill Vogler of Lisco shared knowledge of the North Platte Valley and pointed out landscape features we would have ignored. Tom Haydon of the Bridgeport office of the Nebraska Department of Natural Resources knows everybody in the Valley and helped us meet important people as well as read a subtle ground.

1

Introduction

For a period of about week in early 1865, the Civil War swept across western Nebraska, focused on the valley of the North Platte River (see Fig. 2.1). The fighting that marked this event barely compares to the massive campaigns and terrible carnage that marked the conflict that was taking place in the eastern states. It did not even compare with the fighting that involved Confederate and Federal forces in the American southwest and other portions of the war in the Trans Mississippi West. Indeed the conflict in Nebraska saw essentially no Confederate involvement. The adversaries were disaffected Native fighters and U.S. Volunteer cavalrymen who had been sent to the frontier. Interestingly, the perspectives of the Cheyenne fighters was also recorded.

George Bent, son of frontier trader William Bent, who had taken a Cheyenne wife, Magpie, rode with his Cheyenne kinsmen and friends during this fighting (Fig. 1.1). Years later he wrote down his recollections and shared them in widely distributed sources. The fighting contributed little if anything to resolution of the Nation's Civil War although it helped to set the tone and course of the Indian War that developed thereafter. The Volunteers remembered this fighting as "their War" and some young men on both sides were killed in these events. The story of this fighting is worth relating and that is one of the aims of this book. More than merely describing the evidence of the 1865 North Platte Campaign, this volume has another general aim. The North Platte Campaign offers a worthy illustration of the approach and analytical power of modern landscape-based conflict archaeology. We respect the effort and actions of the parties who fought on the North Platte, but our primary goal is to use the material reflections of their actions as means of understanding what they did and refining how archaeology can study the life and death human behavior that is combat.

Like many of the conflicts of interest to modern researchers, the North Platte skirmishes were between culturally different opponents. In later pages we will review the details of the campaign, but in simple summary, the fighting began on 4 February 1865 and lasted until shortly after the 10th. There were two fairly serious engagements, the first at a small waterhole called Mud Springs and the second in a field near the mouth of small stream that no-one any longer calls Rush Creek. There were probably far fewer than 1000 fighters involved in those skirmishes, but before, after, and between them, they involved several large movements of people and equipment. The equipment the conflicting sides used at these fights is essentially identical to the arms and gear that was in service to other Civil War

George Bent

George Bent, the son of frontier trader William Bent and the Cheyenne Owl Woman was born in 1843 at his father's trading post, Bent's Fort (now Bent's Old Fort National Historic Site, Colorado). He was raised in two cultural worlds, the Cheyenne and Euro-American. He was educated in Kansas City and at Webster College near St Louis. When the Civil War broke out George joined the Missouri State Guard, a southern leaning military commanded by former Missouri Governor Sterling Price. Bent fought in the 1861 battles of Wilson's Creek and Lexington. He was with Landis's Artillery Battery at the March 1862 Battle of Pea Ridge, Arkansas. After Pea Ridge his unit was converted to an artillery unit of Missouri Confederate units. Bent was present at the Battle of Cornith. Shortly after Bent either deserted the Confederacy or was captured by Union troops. He was returned to St Louis and spent a brief time in Gratiot Street Prison but, due to the prominence of his family in the western trade, he was released and allowed to sign an oath of allegiance. He then returned to his southeast Colorado home. He joined his mother's band of Cheyenne, preferring their ways to that of a fur trader.

Bent was present in Black Kettle's village when it was attacked by John Chivington's Colorado Volunteers in 1864 and was so effected by that event he joined the Dog Soldier Society and fought with them through 1867. He is believed to have been present, or actively participated, in 27 Cheyenne war parties or fights, including Mud Springs, Rush Creek and the 1866 Fetterman Fight near Fort Phil Kearney, Wyoming.

In 1867 Bent became an interpreter for the Cheyenne and U.S. Government. He maintained that role for many years. He married Magpie, Black Kettle's daughter, who died in 1886. Afterward he married two other Cheyenne women. He had a total of six children.

In 1901 Bent met and began a collaboration with anthropologist George Bird Grinnell and shortly thereafter with George Hyde (1983). Although not realized in his lifetime Grinnell's and Hyde's books on the Cheyenne are largely the result of Bent's knowledge of the tribe and the many Cheyenne Bent knew and who he encouraged to communicate with both Grinnell and Hyde. George Bent succumbed to the flu pandemic in 1918 at Washita, Oklahoma. For further biographical details of Geroge Bent see Hyde (1983) and Halaas and Masich (2004).

Fig. 1.1 George Bent and Magpie (courtesy University of Colorado Library Archives, Bent-Hyde Collection)

era combatants. They also seem to have used approaches that were typical of America's western warfare.

When this fighting was over and the sides had parted, the combat moved away. War between the U.S. Army and Native Communities was hardly ended, but it was over in this portion of the North Platte valley.

Conflict archaeology and the North Platte Campaign

Conflict archaeology has emerged as a modern discipline with a strong conceptual and popular base. Investigation of battlefields exposes events and places that evoke curiosity and deep cultural meaning. Archaeological study of combat also addresses momentous human behaviors. Among other approaches, microhistory has encouraged archaeologists to recognize the closely rooted connections that link very specific activities and broad trends of human development. Battlefield research developed out of anthropological and historical archaeology, but as it has been pursued around the world, it has embraced a range of theories, methods and a distinctive suite of techniques. Finding the debris of conflict and assessing it in behavioral terms have exposed the history of weapon technologies and political evolution (Keeley 1996). Archaeological investigation has exposed unrecognized conflicts of the past and clarified historic events that were either unclearly recalled or differently interpreted. Archaeological research has also supported memorialization, celebration, and preservation of sites and conflicted landscapes that have been deemed worthy of recognition. Archaeological investigation of battlefields has led to conceptual and technical growth in the discipline. Identifying the artifacts of war has presented conflict researchers with a welter of technical challenges, but interpreting and understanding battle debris in behavioral terms is an even greater challenge.

By their nature, military activities have to take place in regional space. Before serious combat can take place, arms and other resources have to be assembled. Skills have to be developed; Forces arranged; operations organized; and adversaries have to be met. All of those activities are impacted by cultural and natural environments and that means that conflict archaeology is well suited to the approaches of landscape archaeology. Finally, addition to its internal conceptual growth, battlefield archaeology has also found interpretive structures that speak directly to the combat. Military theoreticians have developed conceptual tools to plan and conduct military activities. This body of vocabulary and concepts describes military activities and deals directly with the tools and actions of combat. For those reasons they fit well with the interpretive challenges of battlefield archaeology. Like any ethnographic information, these sources must be used appropriately, but they offer specific insights that can speak directly to the relationship between conflict debris and the behavior that created it.

The North Platte Campaign offers a good basis for the application of landscape approaches to conflict archaeology because of its scale. This fighting is both easily approached and encompassed. The brevity of the conflict and the fact that the North Platte region has been developed into stable agricultural terrain means that archaeological evidence of the Campaign has survived with good integrity. Once rediscovered, these battlefields are much as they were when they were created. The landscapes around them are still open and not massively rearranged. As the research reported here was underway, highly detailed Light Ranging and Detection (LiDAR) imagery acquired as part of a surveying network of Nebraska's water resources spread up the North Platte and made assessment of the battlefields and their contexts excitingly accessible.

The chapters that follow present what is historically known of the Campaign – the importance of the area as a focus for traffic along major trail routes; the military background to the brief but intense conflict; the protagonists; the location of the various skirmishes; and the course of those engagements as described in historical sources and eye-witness accounts. The concept of 'battlespace' and a 'Levels of War' model, recently adapted from modern military tactical operations to the analysis of past conflicts and archaeological data, are introduced along with other recently developed methods of and approaches to the analysis of battlefield archaeology. The field evidence for the identification of the actual sites of the two most important battles at Mud Springs and Rush Creek is presented. The distribution of relatively scant and scattered archaeological remains on a battlefield site can tell only a very partial story and so we combine the physical and historical evidence with topographical analysis and a consideration of the likely tactics and strategies employed by the adversaries in order to develop a more holistic understanding of the battlespaces of the North Platte Campaign.

2

Landscapes and dynamics of the Platte valley in 1864 and 1865

Forms and features of the Platte valley landscape

Modern Midwesterners do not like to hear their area called "flyover country" because it seems to suggest that crowded areas to the east or west are more interesting, attractive and important. Even in 1864 and 1865, however, most Americans could reasonably view western Nebraska as a "pass through" zone. It was a region travelers crossed on their way to somewhere else. The Platte valley offered travelers going west or east a nearly straight route across the central Plains. For most of them, the valley's relatively flat expanse might seem to blend well with the broad lands that surround it. In terms of topography and landscape, however, the Platte valley is a rather complex corner of the Central Plains and its complexities influenced the military undertakings that occurred there.

The Platte River is formed by the confluence of two major water courses, the South Platte and North Platte Rivers and flows along a broadly looping course east to debouch into the Missouri River which forms the state boundary between Nebraska and Iowa. Between them these three watercourses effectively bisect the entire State of Nebraska. Viewed from the west this confluence is a "meeting" that points rather directly toward the east. From the east, however, it is a separation that divides a clearly defined swathe across the Plains into northern and southern routes (Fig. 2.1). The confluence takes place gradually over a section of braided and parallel courses in Keith and Lincoln counties. It is rather arbitrarily marked today by the modern city of North Platte. Historically it was associated with Cottonwood Springs Station (1862), later renamed Fort Cottonwood and then Fort McPherson (now the site of a National Cemetery). The reality is that travelers along the Platte valley would have seen little variation over the 150 miles (240 km) or so between Fort Kearney and the location of modern Ogallala. West of that point the North and South Platte Rivers begin to point in their separate directions and take on very different characters.

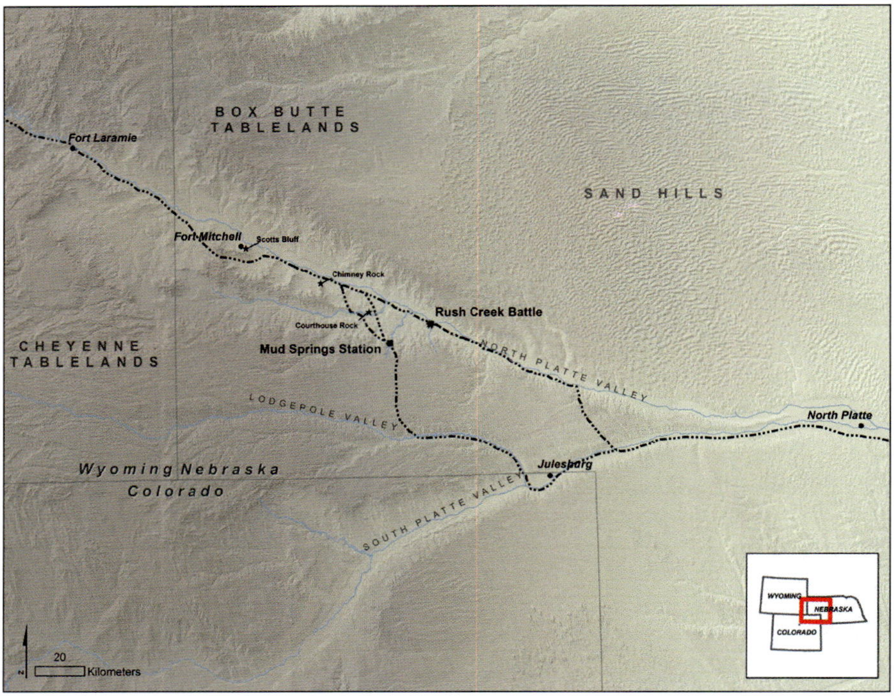

Fig. 2.1 Map of North Platte Campaign region of Nebraska showing the overland trails and military posts along the trail in 1865 (map by the authors)

The South Platte rises as a series of mountain streams in central Colorado and enters Nebraska from the southwest. Once out of the mountains, the river crosses flat-lying plains. Its valley is not markedly separated from the lands that surround it. It is quite flat and in the past may have supported small stands of trees. It is rightly thought of a Plains river.

The North Platte River presents a more complex landscape. It flows in a great sweep across southeastern Wyoming and the Nebraska panhandle. Fed by mountain runoff, the North Platte maintains a rather steady flow, but with an annual precipitation of 14–18 in (*c.* 36–47 cm), the region it crosses can only be described as semi-arid. Away from the river, the valley is generally dry.

To reach the confluence with the South Platte, the North Platte cuts through a series of geological deposits that define and isolate its valley. Exposed bedrock forming the north and south sides of the valley is assigned to the White River and Arikaree groups. It is composed mainly of soft, mostly light colored sedimentary rocks. In many areas the stone layers form steep, even rugged bluffs, but in others the strata are interspersed with wind and water deposited sand, silts and loess (Swinehart *et al.* 1985; Swinehart and Diffendal 1995). With its distinctive set of environment characteristics, the North Platte valley is composed of four separate regions (Diffendal 1993).

The River course

The central core of the both the South Platte and North Platte valleys are the rivers themselves. The size and character of the North Platte River has changed in recent years, but even with the reduced flows that have resulted from intensive irrigation, the river flows across a broad swath of flat-lying land (Fig. 2.2). Whatever its state, the river course is easily approached since it does not lie in a deeply incised channel, in fact, this stretch of the river is the most easily traversable part of the valleys. Crossing the river without a bridge would, however, be a challenge in any season. At times of low water much of the river course is a swathe of loose fine sand. At times of high water the same area is characterised by a swift current that might be several feet deep. In winter, the river course may be covered by a broad sheet of ice. Gallery forests and thickets that grow along the modern river appear not to have been present in pre-modern times. The lack of vegetation may have helped make travel along the river course easy, but it also meant that travelers had few sources of fuel in this part of the valley.

North Platte valley-side slopes

The floor of the North Platte valley is formed by moderately sloping land that reaches from the edge of the river to the base of the bedrock escarpments that define the valley (Fig. 2.2). As noted, land adjacent to the river is quite flat. Most of the streams that cross the valley sides enter the river as shallow meanders that can be easily crossed. The flat regularity of lower portions of the valley sides made it attractive to early travelers. The Mormon and California and Oregon Trails, which together form the major overland trail, ran along the south side of the river very near the edge of the water. This flat, open space also afforded travelers a broad view blocked by neither terrain

Fig. 2.2 The broad sweep of the North Platte Valley is seen here. Land adjacent to the river is relatively flat. Lands to the south rise slightly in a series of ancient terraces, while the land on the north side of the river is the base of bedrock escarpments that help define the valley (photo by Peter Bleed)

nor vegetation. Even travelers beyond eyeshot could often be seen by the dust they raised. This is because fine sands and silt in this part of the valley are easily disturbed when the light grass cover is interrupted. In technical terms, the valley-side soils are assigned as Valent soil. They are composed of eolian sand and loam weathered, washed and blown off limestone outcrops on the valley margins. These soils do not hold water well, thus they are dry and susceptible to wind and water erosion. They are also soft and easily dug (1985 Soil Survey of Morrill County, Nebraska, Natural Resources Conservation Service, US Department of Agriculture).

Away from the river, the valley-side slopes rise slowly to become rolling and much less regular topography. They are transected by a number of small spring-fed streams that flow year round to the river. Along the way to the river these streams meander and weave around topographic irregularities. Some of the streams have formed cuts that may be several feet deep along the side slopes, but as they approach the river they meander in shallow cuts. They tend not to offer straight routes or open views across the valley. Near the bedrock escarpments, the valley-side slopes have many ridges and even substantial hills. These features are formed by outwash from the escarpment or sediments eroded from subsurface bedrock remnants. Some high areas are capped with layers of loess no older than the late Pleistocene. Whatever their source, the irregularity of these land forms means the valley's sides are broken and even hilly. Today, much of this ground can be cultivated with central pivot irrigation, but in pre-modern times, it was sparsely grassed terrain that would be hard to cross in a straight line. A traveler in this country has a very limited view.

North Platte bluffs

Visible stone outcrops are the most dramatic feature of the North Platte valley. The most famous of these are free standing stone towers or buttes like Chimney Rock and Courthouse Rock (Fig. 2.3) that have become famous landmarks. Longer – if less dramatic – stone bluffs extend along most of both sides of the Valley (Fig. 2.4). The outcrops are highest and most dramatic to the west, but they continue nearly all the way to the confluence with the South Platte. Stone in the outcrops is mostly light tan colored soft siltstone and sandstone. Where are not buried or interrupted by erosion, the outcrops form steep bluffs. Some of these, especially on the south side of the Valley, form overhangs and rock shelters providing attractive camping sites, especially for Native American communities in the past. They are rugged and can reach as high as 100 m (*c.* 340 ft). Such steep faces would be challenging to climb or descend, but the bluffs are regularly breeched by side valleys that have milder slopes. These would be beyond the reach of wheeled vehicles, but they would not be a serious challenge to a traveler on foot or horseback. The bluffs were also relatively well-watered since, especially on the valley's south side, many flowing springs are located near the bluff base. Since these springs run continuously they supported stands of small trees. Thinking strategically, if shelter, water and wood were not enough, a camp at the base of the bluffs might be selected because it could also offer a truly sweeping view of the valley. Whether looking for game or potential enemies, an observer near the bluffs could track a large area.

Plains

Beyond the stone bluffs, the North Platte valley is surrounded by rolling Plains. These extend south, becoming the basic setting for the South Platte valley. Geologically, this area is composed of silts, clay, and sand and it is up to several hundred feet higher than the valley. There are few water sources outside of the valley and the available rainfall supports only short grass. This can make the Plains attractive to some grazing animals for at least part of the year, but for travelers, crossing the Plains can be a dry, windswept journey. Just a few miles north of the North Platte valley lies the western portion of the Sand Hills, a huge area of stabilized sand dunes. This expansive rolling country supports few trees and has few streams or rivers, but high water tables between the dunes support large grassy expanses of subirrigated pasture and natural wetlands. This made the Sand Hills attractive to grazing herds and Native communities. Travel in the sandy soil was difficult for wheeled vehicles, but less challenging for Native travelers on foot or horseback.

Trails and traffic patterns of the Platte Valley

Even today, travel to and through the Platte River valleys is largely shaped by the landscape. That certainly was the case in pre-modern times. Given that the North Platte valley featured more geological and topographic diversity, travel in that direction was more influenced by relationships between the Plains and the landforms of the valley. As noted, the easily traveled land near the edge of the North Platte River was the route of the major emigrant trails (see Fig. 2.1). The challenge of crossing the river was enough to keep travelers on one side or the other. Some travelers, notably most of the Mormon companies, stayed on the north side of the river, but the main route of the Oregon Trail and most of the western traffic was on the south (Mattes 1969, 129ff). Whichever side of the river a traveler was on, the challenge was not following the valley, but getting to it since the rocky bluffs had to be crossed in order to reach the flat land at the valley center. Early historic traffic in the valley was limited by the fact that there were few spots where wagons could negotiate the bluffs. The major access and most direct route into the south side of the valley was in the vicinity of Ash Hollow, near the meeting of the Platte's two branches. That approach required a rather long transit across an area of dry Plains and then descent of a very steep slope that came to be known as "Windlass Hill" (Fig. 2.5).

Fig. 2.3 Courthouse and Jail Rocks; typical examples of weathered buttes in the valley area and key landmarks along the overland trail (courtesy of National Park Authority, Scotts Bluff National Park, image in public domain)

Fig. 2.4 Bluff country in the Scotts Bluff National Park (Photo: Magnus Manske, Wikimedia open source copyright)

To avoid that difficult passage, by the 1860s many travelers and the Pony Express system, opted for the so-called "Jules Cut-off," a somewhat longer route that offered easier access to the valley (McDermott 2003, 35). This route stayed near the South Platte as far as Julesburg in the extreme northeast corner of Colorado (see Fig. 2.1). With water stored while crossing the South Platte, wagons could turn north to cross the Plains and enter the North Platte valley east of Courthouse Rock. In this area the stone bluffs are interrupted and the hills on the south side of the valley are cut by streams that make the descent from the Plains relatively easy. An important asset of this route was water provided by springs in the bluff lands. Notably, Mud Springs on Deep Holes creek offered a welcome drink to teams and travelers who had cross the Plains from Julesburg.

Native American travelers faced the same challenges as emigrants, but they had different destinations and simpler technological demands and their communities appear to have been more attracted to the margins of the valley rather than its flat center. Traveling on foot, or horseback or with travois (a

Fig. 2.5 Windlass Hil (courtesy of National Park Authority, Scotts Bluff National Park, image in public domain)

type of sledge to carry goods, consisting of two joined poles pulled by a horse), burdens may have made it easier to negotiate the bluffs. These factors may have freed Native Americans from reliance on the relatively few easy access points so that they could cross the Plains directly to bluff-side camp sites and away from the routes followed by emigrants.

Euro-American trails

Euro-American (ie immigrant) trails offer graphic evidence about the sources of conflict between Native and U.S. Army forces. They were the routes that brought immigrants to and through Indian territory. They also formed the context for the combat in 1864 and 1865 since they defined the course taken by U.S. troops. Trail segments relevant to this story reach from Fort Laramie on the west to Fort Kearney on the east (see Fig. 2.1). Within that range, three specific routes can be recognized. The Overland Trail split near the confluence of the North and South Platte rivers; the North Platte Trail ran toward the northwest on the south side of the river; and the South Platte Trail followed the south side of the South Platte into central Colorado. Both of these trails were well-established and, like most Euro-American routes, aimed at relative flat land near the rivers' edges. Traces such as ruts and fords should remain as documentable evidence of these trails and the activities they supported (Fig. 2.6). The connection between these two trails, known as the Jules Cut-off was the course taken by the Pony Express and many travelers because it offered easy access into the North Platte valley (see above).

Segments of all three of trails were involved in the conflicts of 1864 and 1865. Virtually all the sites and facilities attacked in the closing days of 1864 were located on the South Platte Trail up to 75 miles (120 km) west of Julesburg. As the Native communities moved north after the second attack at Julesburg, Indian forces must have been at least close to the route of the Jules Cut-off. Finally, the North Platte trail segment between Fort Mitchell and Mud Springs

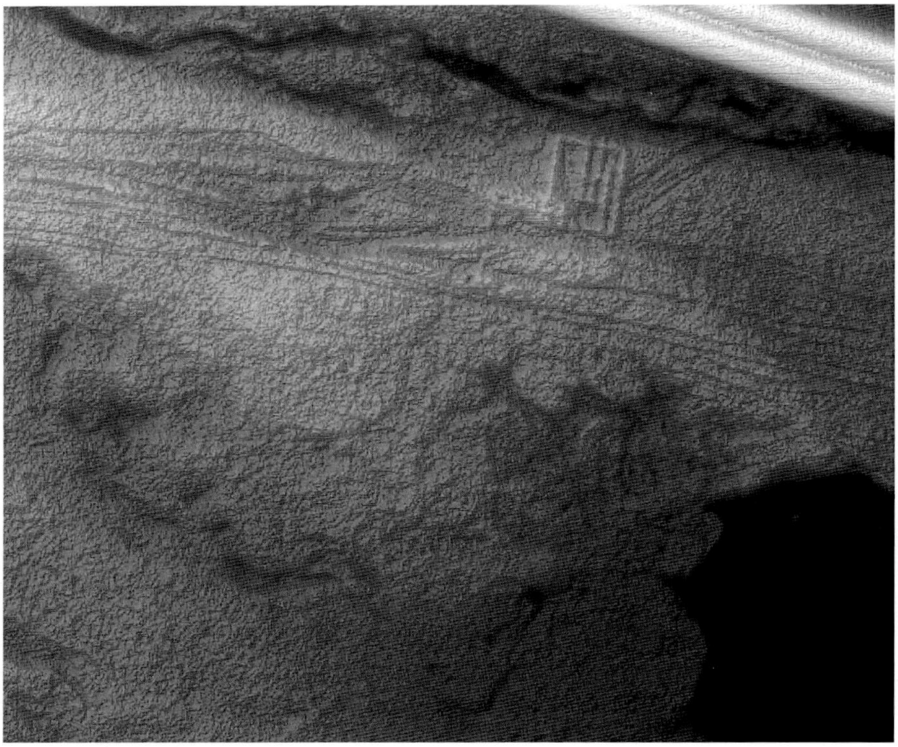

Fig 2.6 A LiDAR derived shaded relief image of Alkali Station, a facility that served both Overland Trail travelers and military units during the 1860s. (LiDAR image created by A. Renner).

was a direct part of the conflict since it was the course taken by U.S. troops to and from their engagements with Native forces.

In addition to using the well-established trails, U.S. forces did some cross country travel. Notably this included Col. Collins's movement east from Mud Springs and then down "Rush Creek" (current Cedar Creek) in pursuit of the Cheyenne community (see Chapter 7). These movements may have followed routes used by Native communities, but they were certainly less well-established than the overland trails. Since they involved a detachment of some 180 horsemen, several wagons, and a cannon, it is possible these journeys required the cavalry to enhance fords or cut banks. Such surface modification should be sought and if they survive in visible traces they should be documented as evidence of the cavalry movements.

Native American trails

Most Native American trails are ephemeral in nature and may not survive in recognizable form. However, oral history and oral tradition presented by G. B. Grinnell (1956) and George Bent (see below) describe the route taken by the Indians. As noted, after combat at Julesburg, the Cheyenne and their allies crossed the Plains east of the route of the Jules Cut-off. Signs of their route may be reflected across the bluffs on the south side of the North Platte valley. There may be archaeological manifestations that exist to identify areas of tribal or band movement associated with the North and South Platte valley conflict of 1864 and 1865.

Army facilities along the trail

In modern military parlance, a "home station" is a permanent location of an active component (see Chapter 3). Reflecting the strategy and operations of 1865, however, by that date, the Army maintained three kinds of facilities along the Trail. These places varied in size but assessing them as part of the 1865 military landscape on the North Platte is critical since they embodied the strategic and operational concepts of the frontier Army. As permanent or semi-permanent bases from which Army forces operated they defined the Army's battlespace, as discussed in later chapters. They defined areas of interest and allowed the available forces to be sent where needed.

Bases

Fort Laramie (Fig. 2.7) and Fort Kearney were major facilities that existed before and after the fighting of 1865. They essentially define the area of the conflict and functioned as supply bases, administrative centers, and staging areas. These major facilities certainly contain features and materials that were shaped by the conflict. Both of these sites should be managed and researched with that recognition.

Fig. 2.7 Fort Laramie, Wyoming *c.* 1858 (F. D. Scott collection)

Fig. 2.8 W. H. Jackson painting of Fort Mitchell as recalled from about the time of the Civil War (courtesy Nebraska State Historical Society)

Forts

Between 1863 and 1865 the Army also established a series of smaller posts that were designated "forts". These facilities had buildings that served as barracks and supply depots. They also had corrals and even sheds and barns for cavalry horses. Few survived long after 1865 but they were certainly integral to the campaigns of that year. They were typically the base for one or two companies of cavalry so they functioned as staging areas from which units could be detached. They had the facilities to sustain deployed forces with logistic, communication, intelligence, security, and other support. On the North Platte, this category includes Fort Mitchell (Fig. 2.8) which was the base of the first relieve forces to reach Mud Springs. Along the South Platte, Fort Rankin (later renamed Fort Sedgewick) was located near Julesburg.

Stations

The most ephemeral of the Army's establishments were described as "stations". The distinction between forts and stations may have been rather arbitrary, but stations may have been more lightly built or were associated with pre-existing road ranches and telegraphic stations. They usually had some type of temporary barracks and corrals so that they could serve as the base for up to a single troop of cavalry. They were distributed between forts and were all closely linked to civilian trail routes. They, thus, offered security to travelers. Troops could also be detached from them. A series of stations was located along the Platte River east of the North and South Platte confluence. The farthest west of these – Fremont Springs Station, along with Alkali Station, and Cottonwood Springs Station (later Fort McPherson) – were certainly involved in the combat of 1865. The several stations in the South Platte Valley were also heavily involved. These included Diamond Springs Station, Antelope Station, and Valley Station. Probably reflecting the fact that most of the action before 1865 was centered in Colorado and Kansas, no stations were established on the North Platte. As important as they were to the 1864 and 1865 conflict, stations present challenges to identification and documentation. As ephemeral facilities, they may not present clear traces. Most were abandoned by the army shortly after 1865. Some developed into post-War bases, Cottonwood Station became Fort McPherson for example. Others morphed into civilian facilities. Finally, the history of the Army stations is complicated by the semantic fact that some civilian facilities – road ranches and stage stops, for example, were also termed "stations." In any case, temporary military facilities played a vital role in the events of 1865, as we shall see.

Native American camps

Native American campsites are the equivalent of modern day permanent Army Home Stations and Army Force Projection Stations (see Chapter 3). The Cheyenne and Lakota as well as other Great Plains groups rarely developed permanent villages in the mid-19th century. Those groups were the embodiment of a mobile hunting lifeway. Therefore, the Home Station concept as envisioned by U.S. Army planners of today has been adapted to the cultural pattern of the Plains tribes for the purpose of this study. Tribal campsites could be large where many bands came together for any number of purposes. Likewise they could be very small, ranging from bands to affiliated family groups out for a communal hunt or simply moving from place to place (See Fig. 4.2 below). Regardless, the camps functioned in much the same manner as Army Home Stations or Army Force Projection Stations during the conflicts of 1864 and 1865. They functioned as staging areas for warriors and as logistical support bases as well as centers for intelligence, security of the family, and in general support roles. Accounting for cultural differences, Native American camps can be categorized and identified as places where communities gathered to create a secure space from which warriors could range out to capture stock and other supplies while, in the present scenario, avenging the massacre that took place at Sand Creek (see below).

Campsites are a significant, if ephemeral, site type that is associated with the North and South Platte valley conflicts of 1864–1865. They provided the anchors by which warriors executed their plans for vengeance and evasion. They were the supply and intelligence base for those warriors, and they were generally placed in locations that ensured their security. Today those sites are entirely archaeological and, as such, the archaeological record is the only evidence of their existence left on the landscape that defines the conflict. Tribal communities were certainly familiar with the territory that was involved in the conflict and probably made use of established camp sites. Archaeological assessment of native camps is aided by the fact that the Cheyenne and their allies are known to have been carrying rich stores of captured goods which they shed as they traveled. These materials provide a key reflection of their involvement in the conflict.

Euro-American civilian facilities

The area of the 1864–1865 conflict was lightly settled by Euro-American immigrants. The great bulk of their activities were concentrated on or very near to the major east–west trails. In fact, at any given time, most of the Euro-Americans in the region of conflict were probably actively moving along the trails. Travelers included both immigrants moving west and freighters bringing goods and supplies to growing western communities. Their movements are reflected in the trails themselves as well as associated evidence of stopping places along them. These could include camp sites, crossing points, and spots selected for mid-day resting or "nooning". With their rich stores, slow moving travelers presented Indian raiders with attractive targets. Several wagons and parties were attacked and plundered between December 1864 and January 1865 (McDermott 2003). These locations are documented only generally, but they may be reflected in archaeologically identifiable features of the potential and real battlespace of the North Platte valley. Travelers may have been the most ephemeral of the participants in the conflicts of 1864 and 1865, but they were truly a significant part thereof.

Overland trail ranches, farmsteads, telegraph lines, and trail stations are terms that describe more permanent civilian facilities that had developed along trails. These facilities are significant by virtue of their association with the initial exploration and settlement of the North and South Platte valley and the development of agriculture and industry. Serving as stopping points on the Overland Trail, as home stations for the Pony Express, and as relay stations for the telegraph, trails stations became among the first permanent Euro-American settlements in the region. Western cattle ranching had begun before the 1860s but many cattle operations – known as trail or road ranches – combined herding with offering supplies and support to travelers.

After 1861 telegraph lines extended along the North Platte Trail and then subsequently along the South Platte route. These lines consisted of networks of small and irregular poles supporting one or more strands of galvanized iron wire. The lines may offer only very ephemeral archaeological evidence of their appearance and location, but they were a fundamental part of the conflicts of 1864 and 1865. Information spread by telegraph brought troops to Mud Springs, and telegraph lines on the South Platte were repeatedly attacked by Indian warriors and repaired or defended by U.S. troops (Ware 1994, 81, 381).

Relations between the United States Government and Platte Valley Native Communities, 1851–1865

The expansion of Euro-Americans across the western United States, and the Platte River's significant role in this process, impacted Native American tribes who considered the area home. Beginning in the 1840s the first sustained contact between U. S. citizens and the diverse groups of indigenous peoples who inhabited the Northern Plains began. This increasing presence of white Americans intent on settlement and exploitation of fur and mineral resources impacted the tribes by gradually constricting their hunting territory and creating intensive competition for game resources among both the tribes and white Americans. The Fort Laramie Treaty of 1851, between the government and representatives of the various Plains tribes, tried without success to restrict the natives to designated geographical provinces and thus remove them from the areas of the principal migration routes. Generally, many treaty promises of the government went unfulfilled. Equally important, specifics of the treaties were often misunderstood by the Indian signers. Some tribes, or elements of them that did not subscribe to the conventions, forcibly resisted the encroachment of white Americans and the troops sent to protect them. Other tribes, in order to advance their particular interests, aligned themselves with the government.

On the Central Plains and portions of the Northern Plains, especially the area presently comprising the states of Colorado, Nebraska and Wyoming, warfare between troops and Native communities mainly involved only a few tribes. Among these were the Lakotas, Cheyennes, and Arapahoe, large groups that played dominant roles in the conflicts with the Army from the 1850s to the 1890s. Both the Cheyenne and Lakota had migrated west, beginning in the mid-1700s, from the prairie region in the vicinity of the Great Lakes, both pushed by neighboring tribes as they sought to contend with white westward expansion. Within decades a Plains Culture evolved based on the horse mounted groups who gave chase to their primary meat staple - buffalo. As white encroachment expanded, it engendered increased inter-tribal and inter-cultural conflict. Elements of some of the tribes moved south or pushed farther west; the Cheyennes and Arapahoes divided into northern and southern groups that retained ties through family marriage and other alliances, while tribes of Lakotas, like the Hunkpapas and Oglalas, occupied remote and isolated parts of eastern Montana. Through inter-marriages, the Northern Cheyennes, Northern Arapahoes, and Lakotas (also known as the Teton Sioux, and composed of bands of Oglalas, Hunkpapas, Minneconjous, Brules, Sans Arcs, Two Kettles, and Blackfeet Sioux) by the mid-19th century maintained strong cultural ties, often living in proximity to each other. These cultural/social connections also proved to be the antecedents of loose military alliances among these people as they contended with neighboring tribes and especially during the later warfare with U.S. troops. As intertribal warfare escalated on the Plains, smaller tribes that found themselves squeezed territorially by larger ones gravitated toward the federal government as a potential means of survival.

Combat along the Platte Rivers, 1864–1865

The Sand Creek Massacre

The roots of the North Platte conflict could be traced very deeply, but the massacre of a Cheyenne village camped on Sand Creek in the Plains of eastern Colorado was the triggering event. The Sand Creek tragedy has been well-studied and much discussed (Hoig 1961; Greene and Scott 2004) so that the focus here can be on ways that the massacre influenced the battles that followed it some 9 weeks later in the North Platte Valley.

Led by Black Kettle, a prominent leader renowned for his commitment to peace, the Cheyenne community massacred at Sand Creek was expecting peaceful negotiations. Anticipating provisions and an extended stay, they had pitched a well-organized camp with a full assemblage of tools and equipment. When they were attacked many of the band's men had left earlier on hunting forays. For that reason casualties of the attack – numbering at least 180 – were mainly women and children. In addition to the human devastation – which included widespread mutilation – the attackers also undertook systematic destruction of the community's equipment and stores. Souvenirs were gathered, shelters and stores were plundered and burned, and horses were removed. The massacre had devastating social and material impacts on the Cheyenne and their allies. The Cheyenne survivors of the Sand Creek Massacre were grievously shaken. Several clans had been decimated (Halaas and Masich 2004, 156). Leaders were being questioned and the community felt exposed to further threats. Most were angry and eager for revenge, but they did not have a well-formed plan of how to react. Finally, the survivors were impoverished. It was early winter and they had suffered great material losses. They faced serious need both for their own survival and to avenge their losses. Sand Creek is now a National Historic Site within the National Park Service system and is listed in the National Register of Historic Places.

Indian reactions to Sand Creek – the move to the North Platte Valley

The Sand Creek massacre presented the Cheyenne with three strategic challenges. First, they needed to secure themselves from anticipated additional attacks. Second, they planned to retaliate for the unprovoked attack. Finally, given their material loss, they had to re-establish the supplies and equipment needed to make it through the winter. Solution of these three challenges did not occur in a simple sequence; they overlapped and harmonized with one another. More to the point, the solution of these complex issues formed the strategic and operational contexts of the battles in Nebraska North and South Platte valleys.

In the days immediately following Sand Creek, most of the survivors sought out other Cheyenne camps on the Smokey Hill River in western Kansas. They spread out to Lakota, Arapahoe, and other Cheyenne communities who provided immediate shelter and support (Grinnell 1956, 174). In short order, the tribe set about assessing their situation. A number of small war parties were dispatched to contact other communities and assess the threat of further attack. These parties reached from southern Colorado to the Platte Rivers and as far north as the Powder River. They spread information about enlarged combat plans to Native groups and gathered solid intelligence regarding the presence of U.S. forces (Hyde 1968, 164ff; McDermott 2003, 12ff; Jones 2005; Henderson 1951).

While this was happening, there was active consideration of how the community should best react to the Sand Creek attack. The massacre dashed any hope of peace and moved the vast majority of Indian leaders and community members toward retribution (Halaas and Masich 2004, 157). The massacre significantly reduced the number of senior leaders and seriously diminished the standing of Black Kettle, who had spoken in favor of peace. He continued to advocate working toward peaceful relations with the Americans, but found few supporters. Survivors included a disproportionally large number of young men who had been hunting and away from the village during the attack. This was the sector of Cheyenne society most likely to be disposed to valorous undertaking (Greene and Scott 2004, 22). The massacre also contributed to the ascendancy of the aggressive Dog Soldier Band which fared well because they had been camped away from the Sand Creek village. Finally, in addition to galvanizing sentiment against White settlers, travelers and the military, the massacre also solidified alliances within and between Native groups. In early December 1864, Cheyenne pipe bearers were dispatched to Lakota and Arapahoe communities inviting them to join the Cheyenne in a war against the Whites. As a result, a strategy of aggressive response against the Americans was established and supported by a solid military alliance.

Tribal leaders selected Julesburg, Colorado as the initial target for their vengeance (Grinnell 1956, 174). Julesburg was a small overland stage stop, telegraph station, and well-stocked trading post on the South Platte (Grinnell 1956, 175) only a mile (0.5 km) from a cavalry base of Fort Rankin. Despite the lofty name, only a single Company of Seventh volunteer Iowa Cavalry was stationed at this fort so it was, therefore, judged a reasonable target by the gathering Native forces. A well-organized party of some 1000 Cheyenne, Lakota and Arapahoe reached Julesburg on 6 January. That night the settlement was carefully scouted by members of the Dog Soldiers Society (Halaas and Masich 2004, 164) and order was carefully maintained until 7 January when an elaborate decoy attack was begun. Fort Rankin was included in the attack and the troops there were tied down. However, the major action happened at Julesburg where a large warehouse and store were plundered and large herds of horses and cattle were taken. Managing the goods that were accumulated in this attack was a challenge that involved a great many families and many horses, wagons and travois. These stores were taken back to the camps in the Republican River watershed of northwestern Kansas.

With a revived larder, Indian forces continued to regroup and organize and develop a strategic response to the challenges they faced (Grinnell 1956,

180). Acting in small units, Indian war groups attacked and sacked other ranches, trading posts and wagons in northeast Colorado. These actions enlarged their equipment store and provided information on the Army actions. Tribal leaders also continued to consider their strategic options. Black Kettle, who had remained with the fugitives of the massacre, advocated pursuing a peaceful resolution to the crisis. That position found only diminishing support and on 26 January 1865, Black Kettle led a party of supporters toward the Arkansas, away from the conflict. The bulk of the tribe and allied groups had decided to undertake what may be styled as another military campaign into the South and North Platte valleys, after which they headed into the unsettled Sand Hills and the Powder River country where they could find allies. This was country they knew in detail (Fig. 2.9).

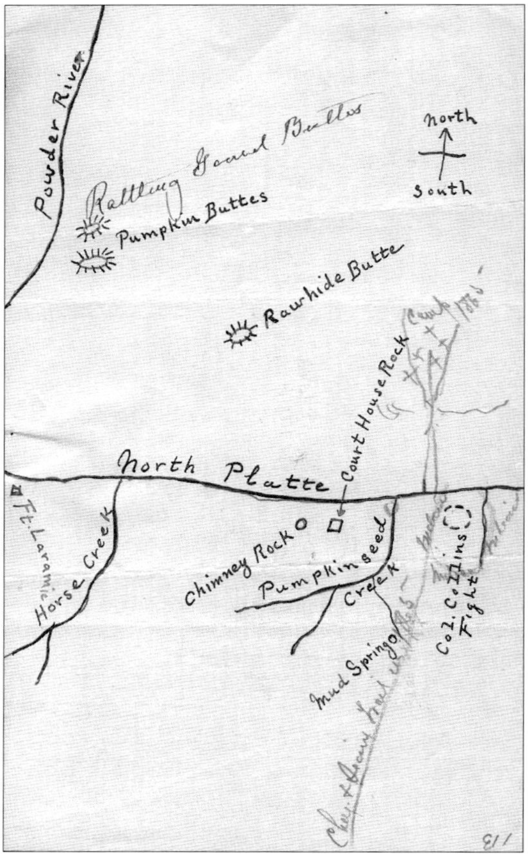

Fig. 2.9 Bent's sketch map of the North Platte Valley noting important landscape features to the Cheyenne and the general area of the trail used by the Cheyenne and the locations of Mud Springs Station and the Rush Creek battle (courtesy of University of Colorado Library Archives, Bent-Hyde Collection)

Posts and ranches the South Platte Valley provided the Cheyenne and their allies supplies and replacement stock. From 27 January onward, Indian forces began to attack these facilities and any wagon trains they encountered as they moved to the north. On 2 February Native forces once again attacked Julesburg, Colorado. They did so in such large numbers that the small Army detachment at Fort Rankin could not come to their aid. The attack was a graphic demonstration of their power, and it garnered another large store of goods and equipment. The nature of the targets of these engagements meant that, in addition to food and supplies packed for transport, Indians were now in possession of many wagons for transporting captured goods and large herds of cattle and horses serving as a "walking larder". Finally, Julesburg and the ranches and wagon trains that were underway in late January 1865 contained many weapons including modern, breech-loading guns. In a 1906 letter, George Bent makes specific mention of the fact that guns were an important part of the captured materials: "All the guns we ever captured were

Spencer carbines. They were the best guns at that time." (Haack 2007, 33–4). The mass of material accumulated in these engagements was so large that managing and transporting it was a challenge. George Bent had never seen a community so richly provisioned (Grinnell 1956, 183; Halaas and Masich 2004, 173). With all of their new gear and many new and unfamiliar conveyances, the Indian party was spread across a "wide and irregular column ... making a trail more than a mile wide." Seventh Iowa Volunteer Cavalry officer Eugene Ware (1994) observed the Indians as they trailed an estimated 1500 head of stock and numerous wagons north from Julesburg after the second attack.

After sacking Julesburg for the second time, the well-armed and heavily supplied Indian community began their move to the north. The multi-band force was solidified and well-organized. By this time, military societies and other operational units had had many opportunities to act together. They were certainly experienced, perhaps even battled-hardened. The Indian community was well-equipped and set on warfare. Heading northwest from Julesburg they crossed the open plain between the South and North Platte valleys. By the night of 4 February 1865, the party had moved into the bluffs country on the south side of the North Platte valley. While the bulk of the party established a camp near the springs at the head of Rush Creek (currently named Cedar Creek), warriors scouting and securing the community's flanks encountered the small detachment of cavalry troops and stockmen ensconced one stream upriver at the Mud Springs telegraph station, near modern Bridgeport, Nebraska.

Army reactions to Sand Creek

Military reactions to Sand Creek were remarkably slow in developing if only because the massacre appears not to have been part of a larger strategy. The perpetrators of the massacre were not in command positions, and the leadership in Denver, Laramie and Omaha did not develop a clear plan for dealing with the results of the massacre. Indeed, some army leaders were incensed and viewed Sand Creek as "horrible murder" (McChristian 2009, 179ff). Major Edward Wynkoop who was a designated agent to the Southern Cheyenne predicted that the Cheyenne and their allies would react with hostility. By early January, Wynkoop had assembled and presented intelligence about Indian presence and plans. He reported that a formal alliance had been established between the Cheyenne, Arapahoe, and Sioux and that a community of 5000–6000 was present in northwestern Kansas.

This information did not lead to changes in military operations along the overland trails. Due to the on-going war operations further east, no additional forces were available, so the Army remained thinly distributed. Operating as they had for some time out of small forts and home stations along the trails and telegraph lines, small units of cavalry continued to patrol the trails. Telegraph lines followed the well-traveled trails along the South Platte and North Platte, but communication did not flow smoothly and units on detached service were often out of touch with bases and other units. In early 1865, the Army was operating much as it had for the preceding years.

The forces that met in the North Platte valley in 1865 were certainly ready for war. The two sides were familiar with one another and they carried many of the same arms. The reasons behind their combat, the processes that brought them to their engagements and the organizations that directed their efforts were all quite different. Strategically, Indian and Army forces were very different, but at this point neither side seems to have aimed at total destruction of the other. Native communities sought security, materials, and war honors, while the mission of the Frontier Army was occupation and protection of transportation and communication routes. Combat with neighboring societies was a standard part of life for Native communities of the Plains.

3

Conceptual tools for the consideration of conflicted landscapes

To study the past, archaeologists need tools that can support the collection and interpretation of material evidence. Some of these tools are physical – shovels, pencils and surveying instruments. Others can be described as technical because they involve manipulation of information that is relevant to archaeological questions. There are also conceptual tools that organize ideas and present interpretations. There is no hierarchy in this array of tools. Indeed, one of the great joys of archaeological research is the mixture of activities it involves. Moving from physical effort of digging and discovery to data recording and display, and then on to the explanation of patterns apparent in the material record keeps archaeology satisfying and stimulating.

As archaeology has expanded and begun to address new topics like conflict and battle, the archaeological tool kit has also expanded. Distinctive material evidence like combat debris requires a special set of descriptive and analytical methods. Conflict researchers have, for example, had to learn about the guns and ammunition used by various past armies. The archaeology of combat and military activities has been supported by distinctive new technical approaches. Systematic metal detection keyed to Global Positioning Survey (GPS) techniques, for example, has become an effective tools for discovery and assessment of combat debris (Scott *et al.* 1989; Scott and Mcfeaters 2011). Firearms identification techniques developed by law enforcement agencies is another tool that has proven very useful for understanding battlefields (Scott *et al.* 1989). The special focus of this chapter is discussion of conceptual tools that can help archaeologists understand the behavior and spatial organization of military events.

Levels of war

Consideration of conflict sites is new enough that archaeologists do not have a refined vocabulary or conceptual inventory for the study of warfare. Anthropological treatment of war and combat offers useful insights (Turney-High 1991; Otterbein 2009; Keeley 1996) into how military events are organized, but a richer source of insights into the range of actions involved in undertaking combat is the modern military. Military theoreticians have developed ways of describing and guiding military actions. Those approaches deal directly with weapons systems, combat and fortifications so are by definition directly relevant to archaeological analysis of battlefields and other military sites. Many discussions of military theories have also been prepared as training aids. Such presentations are concrete, explicit and accessible. Archaeologists have often adapted ideas from other fields so archaeological use of military ideas can follow a familiar pattern.

The U.S. Army maintains a regular series of training publications designed to train personnel in specific tasks and activities. To help individual soldiers appreciate their roles in broader perspectives and to guide senior officers in execution of broad actions, some Army manuals offer clear conceptualization of the range of activities involved in organizing and conducting combat. This literature is particularly applicable to archaeological assessment of conflict because it addresses the connections between individual and small group actions and the general formation of military policy.

Field Manual *FM3-0, Operations (Department of Army, June 2008)* offers a clear and convenient example of an archaeologically applicable treatment of military activities. *FM3-0* is a capstone text aimed at officers about to enter active service. To help commanders visualize the wide range of operations involved in the military mission, current doctrine *FM3-0* presents war in terms of three levels: the *strategic*, *operational* and *tactical.* To emphasize that military actions are interconnected, *FM3-0* presents these levels and the range of activities undertaken by the military as tiers in a graphic model composed of three hierarchical layers (Fig. 3.1). This arrangement emphasizes the conceptual relationship of the range of activities undertaken by the military, but differentiates actions by their contribution to achieving objectives.

Fig. 3.1 Levels of War model adapted from FM3-0 (authors' redrawing)

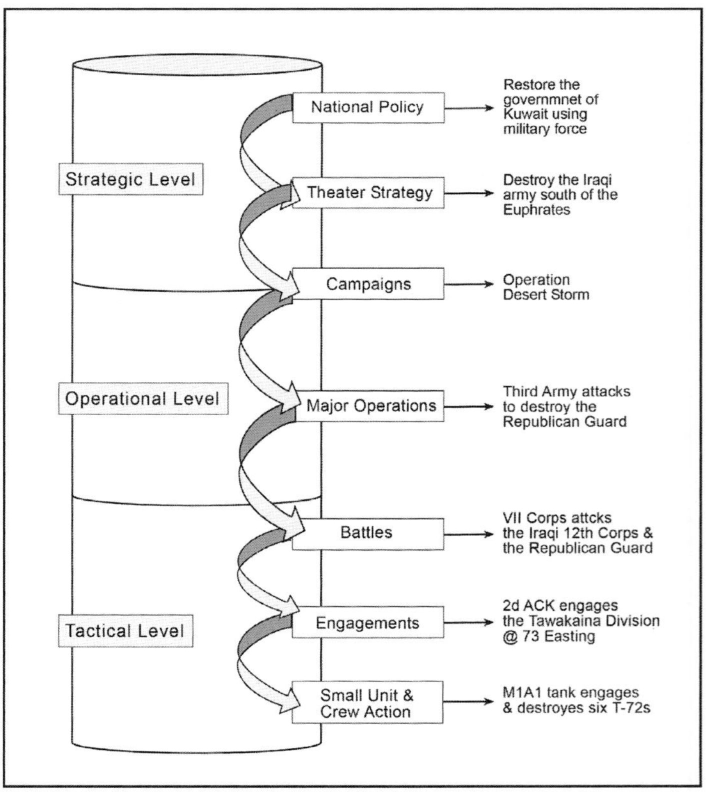

Levels of War

The strategic level

Strategy refers to prudently developed ideas for using power to achieve communal objectives. In military terms, the highest strategic level is formed when political groups determine objectives and develop plans for employing the power available to them to achieve those objectives. Drawing on those ideas as policy, military leaders develop strategic plans for military actions in general and, with specific adjustments, and to operations in specific times and places. In scale, then, strategy ranges continuously from the lofty goals and intentions to regionally bounded applications of those same objectives.

The operational level

Turning strategic policy into specific action is the operational level of war. This is the sphere of conceptual and practical work where field activities are planned, conducted and sustained. It is directly relevant to archaeological investigations since activities at this level are bound to specific times and spaces. Many of the terms and concepts developed to address those temporal and regional frames have potential archaeological applications.

The tactical level

Tactics are the employment of force in combat and the tactical level of war is the realm of direct, close fighting. This level of war deals with how opposing forces use the resources, information and locations available to them to defeat or destroy their enemies.

The Levels of War model presented in *FM3-0* is of course entirely generic. It offers a general frame for investigating organized combat and other military activities. The resources of modern armies are vastly different from those of past military forces, but the issues identified by the levels of war model are general. The strategies that have guided past wars have obviously been diverse and different from one another or modern methods, just as the tactics and weaponry used by past warriors have been highly diverse. What the levels of war model provides is a context for discovering and organizing information about past military endeavors.

Conflicted landscapes as "battlespace"

Conflict does not happen in the abstract. Whenever war happens, combatants have to organize, train, arm and meet so that preparation and movement are central parts of warfare. The scale of the preparation and the amount of movement may vary, but they are always part of combat. From an archaeological perspective, combat always creates more than a battlefield. War always involves places were actual conflict occurred, but also an array of other sites, facilities, and places that were involved in the setting up of, or resulted from, the combat. Landscape archaeology (Ashmore and Knapp

1999) offers a basic approach for conflict research since it provides a general background for the discovery and assessment of places associated with any activity including conflict. Using that approach together with the wonderful new tools of Geographic Information Systems (GIS) provides a powerful means of examining contested terrain (Tipping *et al.* 2014; Foard and Curry 2013; McNutt 2014).

Looking beyond those archaeological approaches, military theoreticians and trainers have developed an interpretive frame for archaeological consideration of for spatial aspects of war. That concept is "battlespace."

Compared to concepts like strategy, logistics and command, the military concept of battlespace has had a brief and even spotty history. The term became part of military discourse and doctrine in a single generation. It seems, too, that during its brief history, military theorists have used and defined battlespace in different ways. Military leaders, like so many others of the modern world, are continually looking for useful new approaches and effective ideas so the dynamic history of the battlespace concept is hardly surprising. It may even mean that the concept is not a particularly useful operational tool for planning and carrying out military operations. Still, as battlespace has been presented in some of its permutations, it seems like a theoretical tool that can have utility for archaeologists studying the record of past combat.

Although the term had been finding utility without specific definition for some time, presentation of battlespace in the 2001 edition of *FM3-0* made it tangible and a part of the Army's training. Military operations reflect strategic priorities that, presumably, reflect high level social or political priorities. However strategies are developed, the challenge presented to soldiers in the field is applying the available combat power to maximum effect. Command is exercised at many levels, but it always involves arranging forces in the best way possible, taking the right actions, and allocating available resources appropriately. As an introductory training manual, the 2001 edition of *FM3-0* presented battlespace as a training aid to help commanders make good decision. As presented in *FM3-0* 2001, battlespace is defined as "the environment, factors, and conditions commanders must understand to successfully apply combat power, protect the force, or complete the mission." As a conceptual unit it includes a wide range of variables; geographic space, environmental conditions, forces (friendly and enemy), facilities and information. Battlespaces are spatially specific so they can change with movement or as conditions on the ground develop. But battlespace is more than simply the area where a military force is engaged: it refers to *conditions* that a commander can observe in order to make decisions about how to pursue a military goal. It is something that a commander "visualizes" based on their experience, knowledge and understanding. To enhance the ability to use the battlespace concept effectively, the 2001 edition of *FM3-0* describes battlespace with a series of concrete components that were presented as graphic model shown in Figure 3.2.

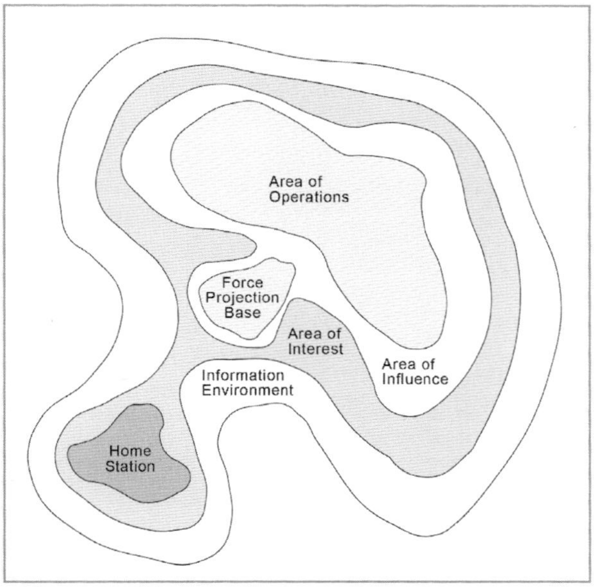

Fig. 3.2 Battlespace depicted as a conceptual model with the important components to successful operations noted (authors' redrawing)

The specific geographic space where a force is engaged is called its *area of operations* or AO. This space may have been assign by a higher command or created by events in the field. The space can also change. However it is arrived at, this space is the center of the area a commander has to consider in assessing a battlespace: but physical space is only a part of battlespace. As the zone where forces are located, it is occupied territory. Around that immediate operational area, the battlespace approach encourages commanders to visualize an *area of influence*. This may not be completely occupied, but it includes the wider zone within which an operational force can effectively project force. It is in their control. Beyond that zone, a battlespace includes an *area of interest.* This area is interesting to military leaders in part because it might include potential objectives for the occupying force. It could as well be occupied by enemy forces. It may not be actively contested, but it is certainly not controlled and is imperfectly understood. Using this zone to get information about enemy forces is an important challenge in appreciating a battlespace. Information on even broader areas, called the *information environment* can also shape events in a battlespace. Information is central to the battlespace approach. It implicitly assumes that, following strategic priorities, command decision will be shaped by the available information.

Facilities can be central features of military operations so battlespace is also shaped by deployment of resources, forces and military facilities. In fact, to illustrate this point, *FM3-0* builds a couple of facility types into its presentation of battlespace. These include *force projection bases* which are staging posts from which forces can be deployed to an operational area. Forces at such bases can be called in to project combat support to field operations. *Home stations* are permanent locations where forces are based and from which they can be deployed. Obviously, access to support is an important element that has to guide the decisions and movement of forces in the field.

Finally, in discussing battlespace, *FM3-0* shows that field commanders can take actions to influence or "shape" the battlespace that is presented to them. That is to say, battlespace can change and commanders can affect that evolution. Short of simply destroying opponent forces, commanders may undertake operations that are aimed at either improving their AO or enhancing their area of influence. Such operations may not be "decisive." Instead, they may be aimed at improving the likelihood of strategic success. Shaping actions can include improving security, actions that limit enemy capabilities, or gathering information. The immediate goal of such actions is to support a mission by improving a force's battlespace, but they are themselves not expected to be decisive.

The presentation of battlespace in the 2001 edition of *FM3-0* is concrete and explicit. It lays out battlespace as a series of general principles and conceptual categories aimed at helping military leaders make good operational decisions. Time and again, the manual presents battlespace and it components elements as "conceptual." It provides no objective means that commanders can use to identify *areas of interest* or other battlespace features. It offers general rather than specific guidance.

Whether or not battlespace offers useful guidance to commanders involved in multi-national counter-insurgencies that mark 21st century conflicts, it offers a generic approach to consideration of contested terrain. The jargon of battlespace certainly cannot translate completely, but information about terrain, resources and enemies must always have been useful to military leaders. Thus the generic quality of the battlespace model, and the structured conceptual approach it encourages to assessment of contested terrain, may provide a useful analytical approach for cross-cultural, historical and archaeological investigation of combat. The test of all models is their ability to organize archaeological observations and enhance understandings of the behaviors they reflect. Application of the model is the focus of the next chapter.

4

Levels of war and battlespace in the North Platte Valley, 1865

In the last chapter we presented some models that we think can help archaeologists interpret battle sites. This chapter begins to apply those generic models to the forces of the U.S. Army and the Cheyenne and allies who were deployed along the North Platte valley. Our challenge is to see if the models can help us to understand archaeological evidence of the battles they fought.

Levels of war and battlespace among the Cheyenne and allied tribes

Warfare and military traditions of Plains Indian culture have been carefully recorded and much discussed (Secoy 1992; Smith 1937, Grinnell 1910; 1956; Mishkin 1940; McGinnis 1990; McDermott 2003; Monnett 2012) because they were historically and culturally very important. In fact, a levels of war model is rather easy to develop for Plains tribes and is interesting because it shows that military strategy and operational organization served as basic structural principles for these groups (Fig. 4.1).

Unlike village-based agricultural tribes, the Cheyenne, Lakota, Arapahoe and related societies depended on mobility to hunt buffalo, trade, and make use of other widely distributed resources. Mobility, which was an essential pattern of life for groups like the Cheyenne, gave operational support to security since communities had the wherewithal to move in directions and to areas that were removed from conflict. Their "home stations" were tent camps that could move and reorganize themselves in various forms and sizes throughout the year (Fig. 4.2). A well-positioned camp would be set up to be secure. Its exposures and resources could be assessed so that threats could be understood. An organized security perimeter would also be a standard feature so a well-established camp was hardly a precarious target. Still, security had to be a major goal for the Cheyenne and related Plains tribes and serving as security for wives, families, and communities was a central value for males.

Most of the combat involved raids conducted by small groups intent on stealing horses, taking trophies, or revenging a previous affront such as

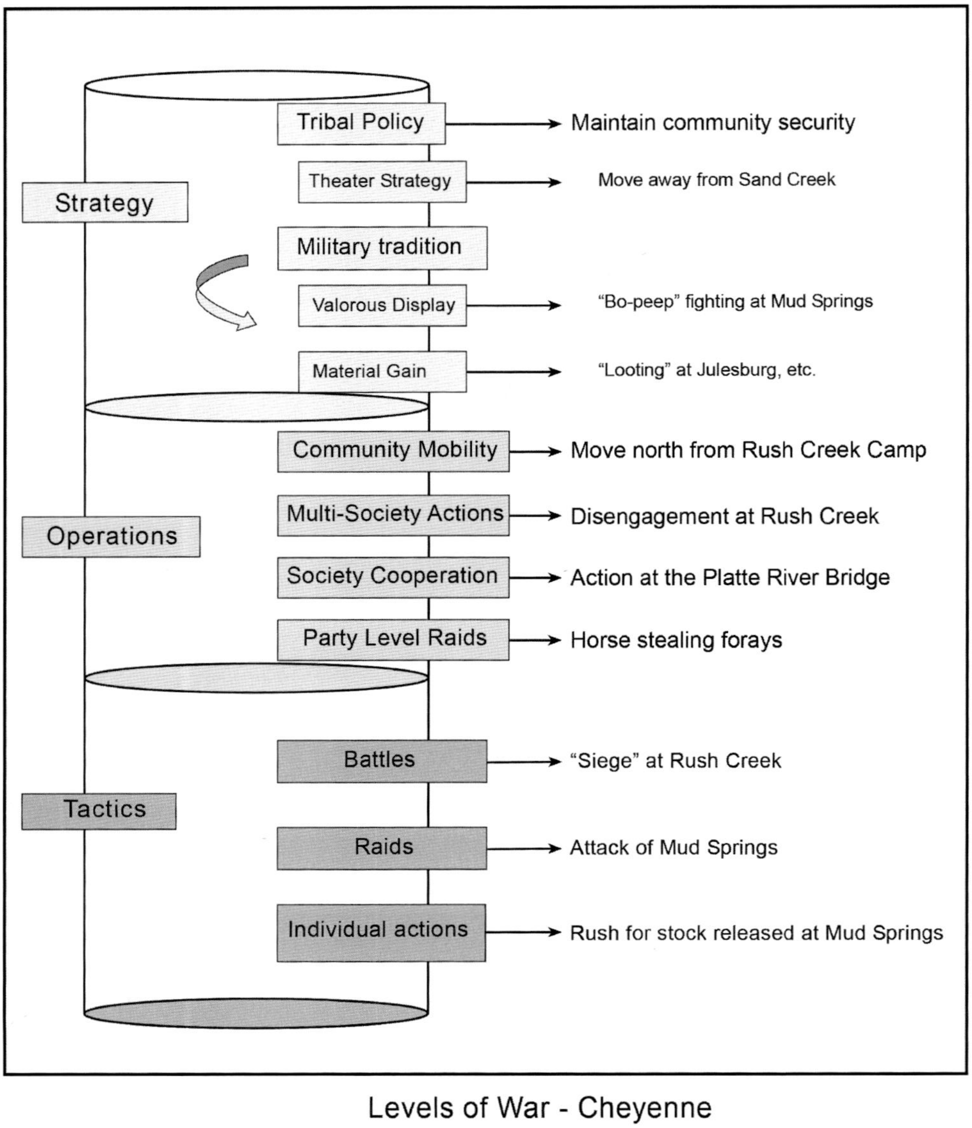

Fig. 4.1 Using a Cheyenne cultural perspective allows the development of Levels of War Model that identifies strategic goals, operational objectives, and tactics for the Cheyenne in 1865 (authors' original)

the killing of a friend or kinsman. Even such small engagements could be very costly, not to mention lethal. They would be particularly threatening to mobile hunting groups like the Cheyenne, who spent much of the year in small, isolated units.

In traditional Cheyenne society, military prowess was the primary source of male achievement. Personal valor, energy, and boldness were the basis of social standing so that combat offered men opportunities to demonstrate or gain recognition. For that reason, individual gallantry that could be observed and socially celebrated in the retelling of war honor events was a major basis for Plains Indian warfare. Trophies such as stolen horses, scalps or captured weapons offered particularly strong demonstration of valor and ability. They

Fig. 4.2 A Central Plains Native American tepee camp photographed in 1875 is in a similar environment to that of the Cheyenne 1865 Rush Creek camp (courtesy Nebraska State Historical Society)

also, of course, carried practical value. Dramatic individual action was, itself, a desirable military goal for Plains Native societies. Valor could be a strategy, but it would be wrong to assume that Plains warfare was foolhardy or careless. Traditionally, raiding parties that lost a member could not return home as victors, even if they had gained honors and booty. Suicidal fighting became a feature of some Plains groups such as a Cheyenne Dog Soldier Society, but it was a late development and a feature of the extremes that developed late in the Indian Wars.

Beyond the search for individual valor and boldness, Cheyenne social organization provided strong and certain support for military operations. The tribe was identified and unified by language and a core of religious beliefs and practices. A group of highly respected men served as chiefs, but residential groups were loosely organized and fluid. The major institutions that bound the tribe together socially were six prominent men's societies. As organized groups, these were called on to serve a variety of social functions. Since they maintained their own discipline and internal hierarchy, members of military societies could organize activities and enforce either secular or spiritual affairs. Their social assignments meant that they were quite used to dealing with a range of activities and "operations" in the strict military definition of that term. Raiding, intelligence, scouting, communications and picket actions were all activities that members of warrior societies were used to undertaking in the normal course of the mobile Plains lifestyle. All of these actions were easily applied in combat.

Practically, the societies were groups of men organized for military operations. They recruited energetic, fearless young men from across the tribe and provided them with operational support. Through mock battles, small raids, other organized actions like target practice and regular recounting of laudable battle exploits, societies trained young warriors. They also placed them in a hierarchy of respect and responsibility through which a man could mature. By providing means for identifying skilled leaders at various levels, societies could organize either very small actions – raids or scouting expeditions – or large military undertakings like frontal attacks or strategic withdrawal. Composed of groups of men who knew one another well and were used to operating together, military societies supported small group cohesion during raids and tactical engagements. By carefully maintaining residual alliances between themselves, groups of military societies could rapidly coalesce into large units that could undertake cooperative actions. The hierarchy within these societies provided an equivalent to the modern military in structure for staff function and disciplined action. Once tribal leaders had assigned a task, or key society members had accepted a responsibility, societies provided clear means for disseminating information. Individual members could be sanctioned, even seriously disciplined, if they did not follow the orders of established society leaders. This led the community as a whole to expect that plans would be carried out. Finally, men's societies provided logistical support for warfare. Members wore distinctive devices and heraldry that could support tactical activities. They also provided networks within which arms could be shared and rationally distributed among men of different abilities and social standing. Sharing a captured weapon was an important means of establishing a close relationship. In all of these senses, then, Plains tribes had strategic and operations organizations that guided their combat.

Tactically, Plains Indian warriors usually functioned as light cavalry. Virtually all men could ride well and were expert in archery and the use of other close combat weapons like the lance or club. But demonstration of combat valor did not, however, require lethal force. Touching an enemy could count as a significant achievement. Such tactics favored individual charges and other small group engagements. By the 1860s, however, firearms were common and familiar to Plains warriors (Secoy 1992, 66ff). When they arrived in the North Platte valley, the Cheyenne and their allies were very well armed with both traditional weapons and breech and muzzle-loading guns. Guns had been obtained through treaty annuity distributions, trade (Halaas and Masich 2004, 162), and captured in attacks on Julesburg, Colorado in January 1865 (see Chapter 2) and raids on civilian and military posts as the Cheyenne moved north from Sand Creek (Grinnell 1910, 174ff). Modern firearms made the Plains warriors truly formidable and changed their military tactics. Guns allowed for effective ambushing and long distance fusillade. They did not prevent the individual engagements of traditional combat, the valiant charges and daring presentations, but they had two other impacts (Secoy 1992, 68). First, they encouraged warriors to work most closely with their terrain and defensive potential it provide. In place of frontal attack in open country, warriors with guns preferred to attack from terrain that allowed a safer approach. Second, where traditional "shock" weapons favored fighting either individually or in small group formations, warriors with guns found success in larger scattered formations.

Levels of war and battlespace of the Civil War frontier army

As explained in Chapter 1, the western frontier was a minor arena during the Civil War. Forces assigned to the frontier were guided by ideas that were not well-formed. Nevertheless, the strategic, operational, and tactical activities of the Civil War Army on the western frontier can be reconstructed (Fig. 4.3).

The Army posted units between Omaha and Denver, and Omaha and

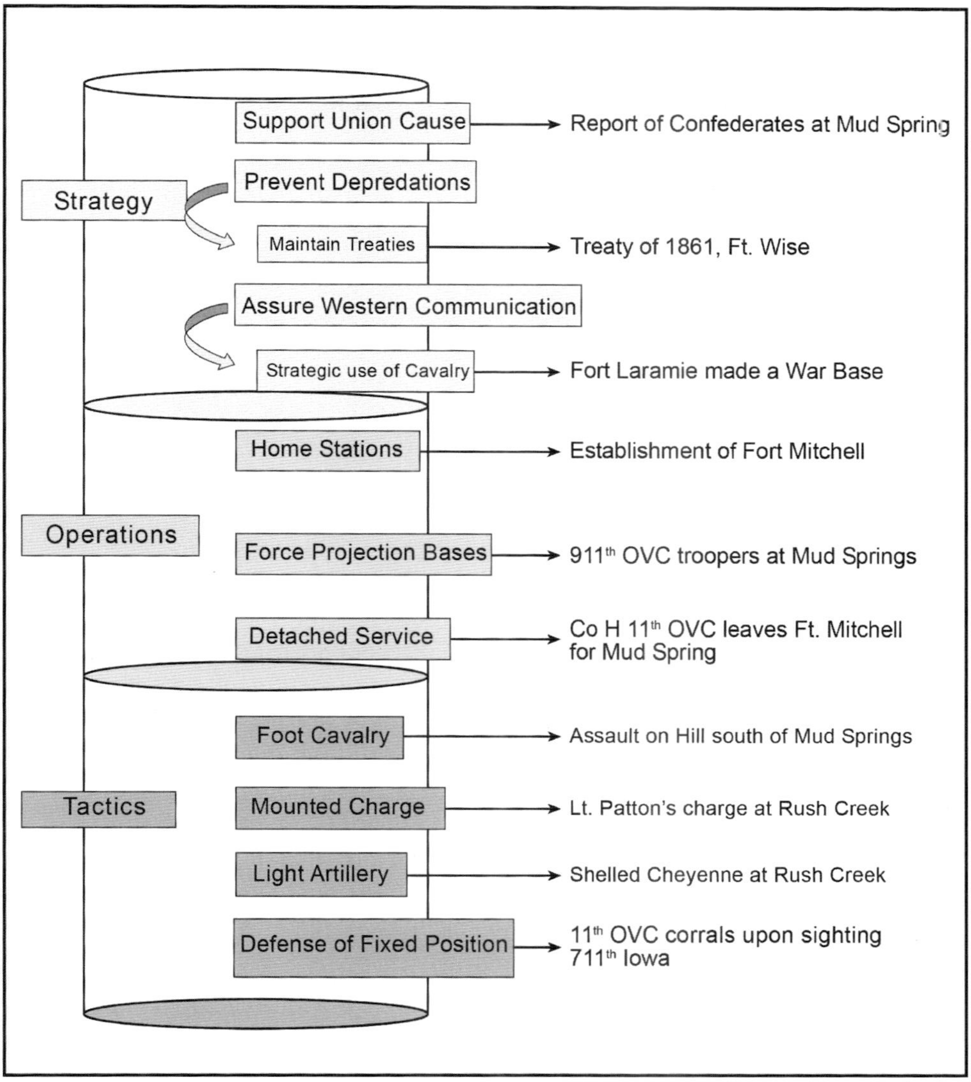

Levels of War - Civil War Frontier

Fig. 4.3 The Frontier Army Levels of War model was developed from historical records and graphically depicts the strategic goals, operational objectives, and tactics of the U. S. Army volunteers stationed at Fort Laramie in 1865 (authors' original)

Washington State, who were there to keep peace and prevent "depredations." The Army units were also posted west of the Mississippi to protect overland trail traffic, mail service and to keep the all-important telegraph operating. One strategy for dealing with Indian conflict involved establishing, enforcing or renegotiating treaties with Native groups. The Army supported these negotiations by either offering security to Indian agents or by having Army officers take part in the discussions.

As a more direct means of preventing conflict with Indian communities, the Army also developed a number of bases on the western frontier during the war. These included existing bases, like Fort Laramie, Fort Kearney and relatively smaller new posts like Fort Mitchell, Cottonwood (later Fort McPherson) and

Alkali Station (Barnes 2008; Hart 1967). Whatever their origins, during the war, these posts served as "home stations" where troops could be based, horses provisioned and supplies maintained. They assured an Army presence on the frontier and allowed military forces to be deployed as needed on short notice. Their distribution was intended to allow forces to arrive quickly at any scene of trouble.

In addition to keeping the peace generally and "preventing depredations" the Army carried the special charge of assuring communication across the Plains. Immigration across the Plains continued throughout the war. The eastern foothills of the Rockies were a focus of settlement at this time and there was growing interest in mining in Colorado and Montana territories. Denver was a rising urban center that needed to be supplied. All of these developments created traffic along the network of trails that formed the "Great Platte River Road." Mail that was vital to the U.S. national interest also flowed up and down the road. By 1862 telegraph lines, supported by regularly placed relay stations, replaced the Pony Express system. Maintaining this communication net and assuring the uninterrupted flow of people, supplies and information was the special responsibility of the Frontier Army (McChristian 2009, 127–35).

Addressing these strategic goals in the West carried distinctive operational constraints for the Frontier Army. As explained, the Army was supported by a series of posts that served as home stations. Some of these pre-dated the War and some survived into the Indian Wars era. Operationally, war-time Army posts had rather narrow goals since they were less involved in regional administration, training or logistics than home bases were to become during the post-war period. Major bases such as Fort Laramie did, however, serve as intelligence gathering centers since they tended to offer residual points of contact between the Army and Native groups. Indian communities nucleated around major bases because they afforded security and access to goods (McChristian 2009). In addition to posts that served as home stations, the Army also stationed much smaller groups of soldiers for very short periods at facilities that required special security. These included telegraph stations where groups of 5–10 soldiers, details, squads or platoon-sized deployments could be stationed, either alone or in company with civilians. Such stations functioned as "force projection bases" (see Chapter 3). Most could be temporary and it appears that none of them was constructed by the army.

Even with a network of dispersed posts and stations, the huge area served by the Frontier Army made mobility a priority. The Frontier Army was composed overwhelmingly of cavalry units, essentially all of them formed as volunteer regiments. In theory, a cavalry regiment was composed of ten companies of up to 80 men each. That organization could afford considerable flexibility. In the East, companies could be amalgamated into squadrons or battalions. Certainly cavalry officers knew how to organize and manage multi-company groups, but on the broad Plains of the frontier, regimental organization allowed for smaller units to be formed. Few bases housed more than two companies and many small posts were home to single or even a partial company. Whatever their size, cavalry units were permanently stationed at a base so that their mounts were stabled or held in corrals, fed on forage and grain and generally well maintained. For that reason, when a crisis occurred up or down the trail, a cavalry unit could respond quickly and with vigor by going on "detached service". Cavalry men were trained to ride intensively, but as organized units so that they could arrive fit and prepared for action. They were equipped to operate for several days without resupply. Cavalry horses became stressed when they had to survive on wild feed. Thus, in addition to provisions and ammunitions carried by individual troopers, a unit on detached service had to travel with pack horses or, more likely, wagons carrying additional food and ammunition and stock forage. With that much capacity, the traveling kit could also include such bivouac equipment as axes, shovels and ropes that might be needed along the way or at an engagement.

The array of arms carried by Western cavalrymen was diverse, but by 1865 most cavalry units had been equipped with revolvers and breech-loading long arms, including even modern seven-shot Spencers. Cavalry units could also travel with 12-pounder Mountain Howitzers. These small brass-barreled weapons could be either drawn by a team or packed on two or three horses. The cannons traveled with an ammunition chest or limber of case shot, shell and canister rounds. Following the recommendations of the 1861 cavalry manual of Philip Cooke, Western cavalry units traveled in a single rank with each mounted rider or horse occupying at least 20 ft (*c.* 6.1 m) (Griffith 1986, 42; 1989). In gross terms, then, a moving single company could be about one-fifth of a mile (320+ m) long. Standard procedure also called for a scouting party to ride ahead of the main force and for flankers to be positions on both sides up to one-quarter mile (400 m) of the column. A cavalry column on detached service was, in other words, a large undertaking.

Tactically, American cavalry units made use of their mobility to move toward engagement, but they usually fought on foot. That is, they usually functioned as "mounted infantry" or "foot cavalry" (Griffith 1989, 184ff; 1986, 42). Mounted charges were part of the Civil War era cavalry tactical repertoire, but even in eastern campaigns, mounted charges were used very selectively. Instead, once a cavalry detachment arrived at an operational area, they usually dismounted and engaged the enemy on foot. Once on foot, cavalrymen might assault an enemy, firing as they did so (Griffith 1986, 42). Alternatively, a dismounted cavalry unit might begin an engagement by establishing a defensive position. This seems to have been an especially common tactic on the frontier where small, out-numbered units patrolled huge areas with incomplete intelligence. Making effective use of artillery required, if not a defensive posture, at least creation of a fixed position. Since bivouac equipment was carried by units on detached service, it would be easy to prepare defensive position with simple earthworks or other constructions. Whichever tactic a cavalry unit adopted, dismounting meant that one rider in four had to be detailed as a horse holder.

Together with wagon crews and others detailed to managing stock, something like a quarter of a cavalry detachment would not be available for combat.

The essential elements of North Platte battlespace – trails and battlefields

Trails were the organizing element in the 1865 battlespace. Trails that brought immigrants to and through Indian territory were the primary reason U.S. troops were present along the North Platte. Force projection bases were distributed along the trail at place like Mud Springs. And with the telegraph and the free flow of travelers, the trails defined the Army's information environment. U.S. forces were able to do some cross-country travel, but most cavalry operations took place along the trails.

Native communities could follow their own traditional routes or travel freely across country. Cheyenne war parties could move across the landscape with great freedom. But points where they might meet Army troops were largely defined by the trail networks.

Generally, skirmish sites in the conflicted area of 1864–1865 were selected by Indians seeking useful supplies or vengeance on travelers, road ranches and farmsteads, and on telegraph and military installations. These engagements seem to reflect confidence the warriors and the bands in general had that they would be successful in maintaining their traditional way of life in their country. Their information environment was huge. And with a well-formed understanding of the area they were crossing the Cheyenne and their allies likely felt that they had an expansive area of interest. By instigating the attack on Julesburg, Colorado and, later, on Mud Springs, the Cheyenne and allied tribes changed their normally defensive tactical posture and aggressively projected a lack of fear of the U.S. troops, as well as disdain for their presence in lands they considered their own. In practical terms, Cheyenne battlespace may have changed radically toward the end of the North Platte campaign. The Rush Creek battle was forced on the Cheyenne and Lakota as they were moving into an area of safe isolation in the Sand Hills. Camped as they were near the trail with U.S. troops near their immediate area of operation, Indian forces adopted a defensive posture. To defend their families and protect their movement out of the valley the warriors were forced to corral and harass Lt Col Collins's forces at Rush Creek. The tactical adjustment served them to achieve a strategic withdrawal from the Platte valleys. After completing their overall goals of resupplying and chastising civilians and military forces, following Rush Creek, they could continue their move toward secure isolation.

5

Conflict begins – the battle of Mud Springs

The nine enlisted cavalrymen who occupied the Mud Springs telegraph station on 4 Feburary 1865 may have felt secure if not completely comfortable. Because of the natural water seep that gave the station its name, Mud Springs was a well-established watering stop for travelers moving along the Jules Cut-off, a shortcut that offered wagons a way around the steep hill at Ash Hollow (see Chapter 2). It had also served as a Pony Express home station but when new technology became available in 1860 it was turned into a telegraph station. The soldiers themselves were experienced frontiersmen having served in the West since 1862. Their regiment, the 11th Ohio Volunteer Cavalry, was headquartered at Fort Laramie (see Fig. 1.1), but had men dispersed in small units along the trail. The detachment at Mud Springs provided security for the telegrapher, Richard Ellsworth, and four stock herders who had a small herd of cattle owned by ranchers Creigton and Hoel nearby, as well as horses and mules in the station corral (*Omaha Weekly Republican* 21 March 1865). This group were aware that some Native American communities had begun fighting with military and civilians, but those conflicts were poorly reported and had been occurring in Colorado over 50 miles (80 km) to the south of the South Platte River.

The detachment assigned to Mud Springs was not yet aware that a large community of Cheyenne, allied Lakota and others had crossed the Plains that separates that two rivers and established a camp less than 8 miles (13 km) from them at the head of a spring-fed creek that travelers called Rush Creek (see Fig. 1.1).

The Indian community probably knew about the station at Mud Springs, but they were heading away from conflicts that had taken place at Julesburg and elsewhere and moving north toward the secure isolation of the Sand Hills. Rush Creek camp site was certainly familiar to the Indian community and they arrived with a substantial store of captured arms and resources that included several wagons and a herd of cattle. Apparently, as their Rush Creek camp was being organized, Cheyenne warriors discovered the forces at Mud Springs. Fighting there began on the morning of 4 February.

Mud Springs as battlespace

An 1864 ground plan sketched by Lt Caspar Collins shows the Mud Springs Station consisted of two log buildings and a corral (Fig. 5.1). One building measured 35 × 16 ft (*c.* 10.7 × 4.9 m) and served as a squad room and telegraph office. The other building was a stable that measured 40 × 20 ft (12.2 × 6.1 m). These buildings were not designed for defense; rather they were built as a working unit on the overland trail system with no thought to a defensive wall

Fig. 5.1 Plan of the Mud Creek Station in 1864, drawn Lt Caspar Collins (courtesy Colorado State University Library Archives, 10217/37595)

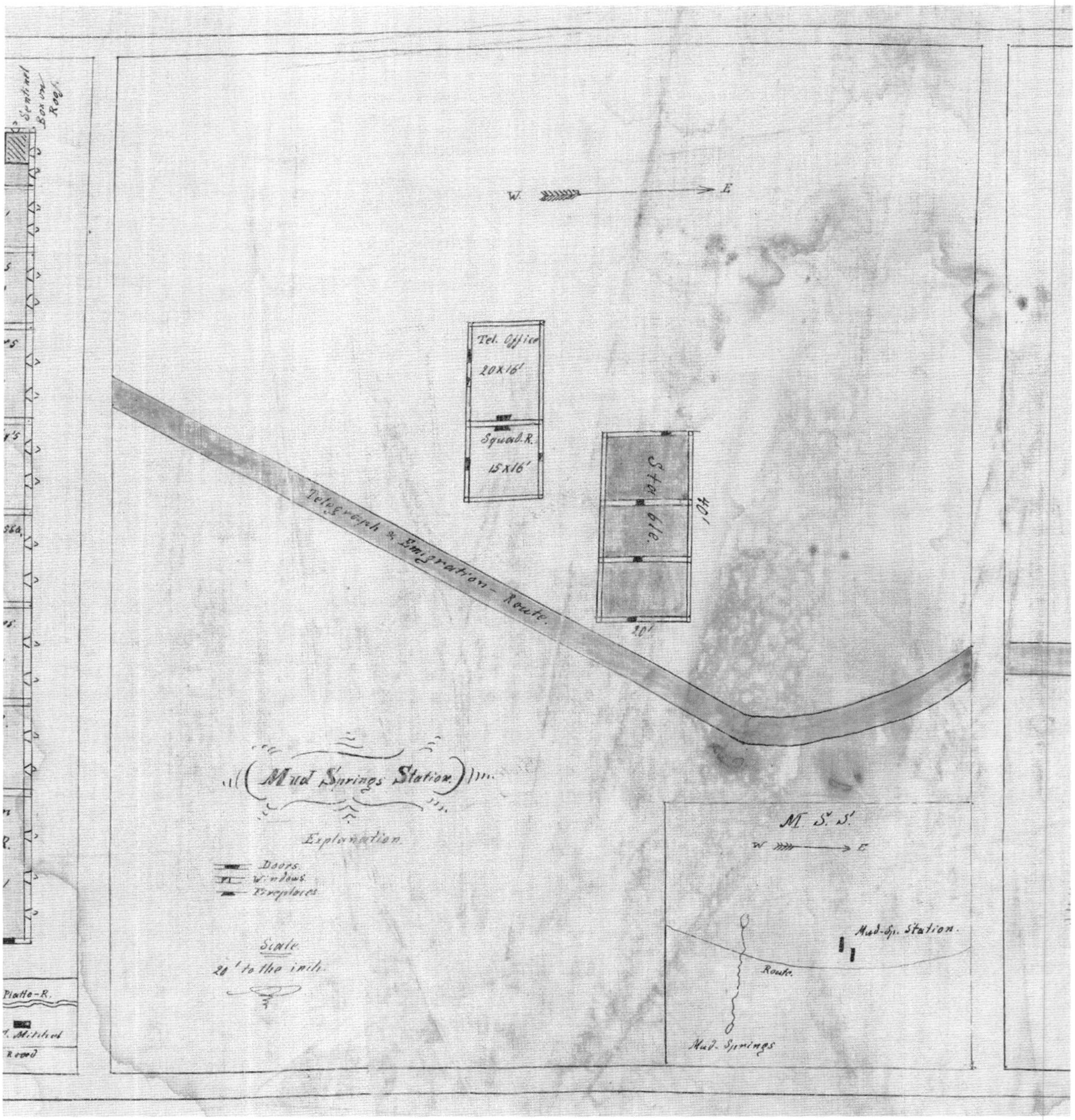

or palisade. The structures sat on the west side of dry wash that served as the path to the watering hole of Mud Springs. The station buildings were on a land surface some 4 ft (1.2 m) above the wash and separated by a low bank. A wetland, possibly blocked to form a shallow pond, formed the northern margin of the station. A corral was located next to the stable, apparently to the west.

Sir Richard Burton, an English scholar and adventurer, who passed through when the site was serving as a Pony Express station on 12 August 1860 described it thus:

> "The station was not unlike an Egyptian fellows hut, made of sod half peat with vegetable matter; it is taken up in large flakes after being furrowed with the plough and cut into proper lengths with a short handled spade. The roof was made of cedar timber. We ate in an open shed next to a doorless dormitory. I spent the night in the body of a dismantled wagon to escape the pests of the infested dormitory." (Burton 1963)

By 1865 the adobe structures appear to have been dismantled and rebuilt with logs as described by A. G. Shaw, a battle participant with the 11th Ohio Volunteer Cavalry (OVC). Shaw stated:

> "There were several buildings, and rooms connected or a part of the same building. The Indians got behind the hill in the rear of the buildings & would crawl to the top and shoot down into the log buildings. There were no windows on that side, but occasionally a bullet went through the chinking and penetrated to the inside, but nobody was hurt." (Jensen 2005, 304)

Located as it was on the Jules Cut-off, Mud Springs was completely integrated into the overland trails network. To both the north and the south, the travelers had access to trails (Fig. 1.1). The main branch of the North Platte trail was about 7 miles (11.3 km) away to the north. Wagon travelers may have felt that the station also offered a broad vista. In fact, a large, high hill a mile (1.6 km) east of the station blocks the view in that direction. More immediately, the station site is surrounded by a variety of smaller topographic features. Immediately east of the buildings there is a broad sandy draw. The level of the station is separated from the draw by a bank that is steep in some areas but less than 4 ft (1.2 m) high. A series of hills is located to the south of the building site. The closest of these is less than 100 yds (*c.* 90 m) away and directly overlooks the buildings. The buildings have not survived, but their location is marked by a stone monument erected in 1939, based on oral traditions.

In his report presented in the Official Report of the War of the Rebellion Collins (*Official Records of the War of the Rebellion*, Series I Vol. 48 Pt I (1886), pp. 88–98, 816, hereinafter cited as Collins Report, OR) described the fighting on the 6 February as a game of "bo-peep" in which both the Army and Indian fighters searched out sheltered spots from which they could stand and surprise their adversaries. The warriors were attracted to horses in the corral. They also harassed the station on horseback and on foot, using the terrain as effective cover to draw close. The fighting spread over a wide area with mounted Indians alternately charging the station and taking shelter from soldiers' rifle fire by galloping behind far hills. The soldiers' weapons, Wesson and Spencer rifles or carbines would have had an effective range of 400–600 yards (365–550 m), although the bullets could travel farther before reaching terminal velocity.

Strategy and tactics of the Mud Springs operation

While the precise number of soldiers and warriors who fought at Mud Springs and Rush Creek is not likely to be known with certainty, the historic records do provide a reasonable approximation for those on the army side. Mud Springs station was occupied by nine soldiers, one telegrapher and four civilian stock herders. The rescue party was composed of soldiers from the 11th OVC and 7th Iowa Volunteer Cavalry (IVC) stationed at Forts Laramie and Mitchell. Historical sources are somewhat conflicting, but according to Orders No. 146, dated Fort Laramie, 4 February 1865, the following numbers of soldiers were ordered on the march to Mud Springs:

Co. A, 11th OVC: Acting 2nd Lt Robert F. Patton and 20 men;
Co. B, 11th OVC: 10 men;
Co. C, 11th OVC: Acting 2nd Lt John M. Herriman and 10 men;
Co. I, 11th OVC: Acting Capt. Jacob F. Apt and 30 men;
Co. L, 11th OVC: 10 men; and
Co. D, 7th IVC, Capt. William D. Fouts and Lt Dudley L. Haywood, and 40 men, and Assistant Surgeon George Zeigler (11th OVC Regimental Returns, NARA RG98, Microfilm copy on file Fort Laramie National Historic Site Library, edited and complied by William Saunders, hereinafter cited as 11th OVC Regimental Returns).

From Lt Col. Collins's after-action report we also know that 1st Lt Theodore B. Harlan and 2nd Lt John R. Moloney of Co. I; 1st Lt Oliver S. Glenn, Regimental Commissary of Subsistence; 1st Lt John G. Reeves, Regimental Adjutant; and Acting 2nd Lt Josiah G. Harrington, Regimental Quartermaster Sergeant) were also present (Collins Report, OR, 92–8). This makes a total of 12 officers and 120 soldiers from Fort Laramie in the initial command that marched to Mud Springs.

Lieutenant Colonel William O. Collins (Fig. 5.2), commander of the 11th OVC and based at Fort Laramie, telegraphed 1st Lt William Ellsworth, Co. H, 11th OVC, at Fort Mitchell to take all available men and go immediately to the relief of Mud Springs Station. Lieutenant Ellsworth, with 36 men from Co. H, 11th OVC, marched to Mud Springs on the late afternoon of 4 February 1865, arriving at around 2 am on 5 February (Collins Report, OR, 92–8).

Orders No. 152, dated Fort Laramie, 6 February 1865, indicate the following additional soldiers were ordered to Mud Springs Station:

Co. A, 11th OVC: 1st Lt William H. Brown, and 5 men;
Co. B, 11th OVC: 3 men;
Co. C, 11th OVC: 24 men;
Co. I, 11th OVC: 15 men; and
Co. D, 7th IVC: 5 men.

This makes a total of one officer and 52 men (11th OVC Regimental Returns). Brown's detachment with a 12-pdr Mountain Howitzer arrived at Mud Springs on the morning of 8 February. It was Collins's orders that created and directed the training of 11th OVC men in the use of Mountain Howitzers and 3 inch rifled Field Guns that the 2nd Battalion of the 11th OVC brought west with them in October of 1863 (11th OVC Records).

Combat at Mud Springs began when upwards of 200 warriors attacked the station and stole stock around 3 pm on 4 February. As the warriors did not cut the telegraph wire immediately the beleaguered soldiers and civilians were able to send for help via the talking wire. In the early morning hours on the 5th, 1st Lt William Ellsworth and 36 men of Co. H. 11th OVC, arrived at the station from Fort Mitchell. When the Indians returned on the morning of the 5th, they were surprised by the increased number of soldiers at the station and only lightly skirmished with them during the morning. They soon withdrew to the surrounding bluffs. Lt Col. William O. Collins arrived with 25 men from the 11th OVC the morning of 6 February. Captain William D. Fouts, Co. D, 7th IVC, arrived that same morning around 8 am with 40 men from Co. D, 7th IVC and 55 men of the 11th OVC. Heavy fighting began soon after Fouts arrival. The Indians, seeing that their opportunity for a victory had slipped away, eventually gave it up in the afternoon.

Fig. 5.2 Lt Col. William O. Collins commanded the 11th Ohio Volunteer Cavalry. His command center was Fort Laramie, Wyoming, but covered a vast territory in Colorado, Wyoming and Nebraska (courtesy Denver Public Library)

By the time of Capt. Brown's arrival on the 8 February the command swelled from the original nine soldiers, and five civilians to 14 officers, 217 enlisted men, and five civilians. It is probable that a number of other regimental staff officers and enlisted men went with Collins who are not otherwise accounted for in the extant orders, but the minimum total appears to be 236, officers, enlisted men and civilians. The disposition of these men cannot be known but, arriving as many of them did with wagons, it is likely that they set up shelter tents and fireplaces. There must also have been a great many horses that had to be closely held in either corrals or on picket line. Clearly over the course of a few days, Mud Springs had become a crowded, perhaps even congested, space.

The primary army accounts are provided in the after-action report of Lt Col. William Collins of the 11th OVC (Collins Report OR, 88–98, 816; Hewett 1997, 203–33; McDermott 2003; 1996). The Native perspective is represented in accounts of the fight left by George Bent, the son of noted trader William Bent, and his Cheyenne wife (Fig. 1.1) who rode with his Indian kinsmen (Hyde 1983, Halaas and Masich 2004; Grinnell 1956; Haack 2007).

When the warriors began their attack the defenders stayed in the station buildings and traded shots with the attackers. Indians attacked both on horseback and on foot. They appear to have been able to approach the station building close enough to fire guns and arrows into the building walls, probably within 50 ft (*c.* 15 m) or so. (Fig. 5.3).

George Bent described the Mud Springs fight in a letter to George Hyde of 4 May 1906. This letter has been cited by several authors (Hyde 1968, 183–9; Halaas and Masich 2005, 174–8; Grinnell 1956), but the original text presented in a transcription by Stephen Haack (Haack 2007, 33–4) presents useful additional information, although Bent appears to conflate the Rush Creek events somewhat.

> "That night scouts were sent ahead reported ranch on Muddy Springs had soldiers, so early next morning everybody got on their best horses and started for the springs. The village turned north east from here. We went due north for the ranch. When we got near we could hear lots of firing. Lot of Indians had started for this place that night so as to run the stock, but soldiers had

Fig. 5.3 A Cheyenne biopictographic depiction of warriors attacking soldiers near a structure provides a sense of the Cheyenne recordation of the fighting in 1864 and 1865 in the Platte Valley (courtesy History Colorado, Cheyenne Sketchbook 10036210)

> all their animals inside the corral. The soldiers were inside of buildings and had port holes to shoot through. We could not tell how many soldiers were in this party. Sand creek ran close to the ranch with high bank. The Indians got behind this bank and shot into the buildings. At noon they turned all their animals loose. The mules and horses ran in every direction. Indians were running after them [Fig. 5.4]. Among rules with Indians, who touched the animal with anything in his hand, the animal was his. I understood the soldiers were running out of ammunition. They turned their stock loose so the Indians would leave them and they did so. After this the big village camped about [he gives no number here] miles east of Muddy Springs where we had fight. No Indians were killed in this fight and as I say we could not tell how many whites were killed in this fight. Lots of shooting was done on both sides. All the guns we ever captured were Spencer carbines. They were the best guns at that time and were handy to carry on horses."

In Lt Col. Collins's handwritten copy of the official after-action report (Collins Papers, DPL) there is a sentence that was redacted in the published copy regarding the number of animals lost to the warriors during the fight. Collins stated the stock lost to the Indians:

> "consisted of one mule & three horses belonging to the Government & ten or fifteen ponies and horses belonging to Citizens & also the cattle herd of Messrs. Creighton and Hoel [sic] which was on Rankin's Creek about four miles distant ..."

Fig. 5.4 A Cheyenne warrior capturing a U.S. branded horse. Such a capture was typical of war honors and war trophies gained by individual warriors during a battle (courtesy History Colorado, Cheyenne Sketchbook 10036202)

This part of the official account of the Mud Springs fight indicated the horses and mules, numbering between 15 and 20 animals were corralled at Mud Springs, but the cattle herd was some 4 miles (6.4 km) away on another drainage. It seems likely the stock herders sought the protection of the soldiers at Mud Springs Station bringing only their horses and mules with them and not the cattle herd, as appears in other accounts.

Army accounts of the Mud Springs combat are more expansive than that of Bent. In his after-action report written on 15 February 1865, Collins seems to present a rather clear set of strategic priorities. In this report he indicated that although communication with the South Platte valley had been "cut off" he was aware of fighting that had taken place at Julesburg and elsewhere along the South Platte. He stated that Indians "in great numbers" were determined to "take the posts upon the North Platte ... and then go north to the buffalo country on the Powder River." He also said that Indian attacks had cut off mail and trail communications from Fort Kearney. Some of this information may have been realized only after his operation was completed, but the report indicates that Collins understood strategic goals of his operation. He was leading a force that was to prevent depredation like the attack that was ongoing at Mud Springs and re-open the overland trail (Collins Report, OR).

Collins issued six special orders pertaining to the organization of his column and the movement of troops to relieve the post at Mud Springs as well as pursue the Cheyenne after the battle was over (Collins Papers, DPL). Collins's Special Order 1 dated 5 February at Fort Mitchell (Figs 5.5 and 2.8) states that the first squadron consisting of a detachment of Company F, 7th IVC was under the command of Capt. W. D. Fouts. The second squadron, made up of a detachment from Company I, 11th OVC, was under the command of Capt. J. F. Apt. The third squadron, a composite unit made up of men from Companies A, B, C, D and L of the 11th OVC was under the command of Acting Lt Robert Patton. Patton's regular rank was Sergeant.

In addition Special Order 1 orders Assistant Surgeon A. F. Ziegler to examine all enlisted men to determine if any are ill or suffering from frostbite. Those men were to be excused from participating in the relief march. The order further notes Collins would take 25 men and march to Mud Springs with the remainder of the command and the wagon train following Collins as quickly as possible. The march orders also required the men march in silence, have proper guards or flankers out and take precautions against surprise attacks.

Moving quickly and riding through two nights, Collins' column crossed the 90 miles (145 km) to Mud Springs and arrived on the morning of 6 February. He had dispatched, but not waited for, a small detachment of the 11th OVC that was traveling with the 12-pr Mountain Howitzer and arrived at Mud Springs in the early morning of 8 February. Collins says that after two nights' march the troops arrived hungry and cold so that the fight was initially "a clearly defensive fight". An overnight ride in midwinter must have been a demanding effort, but the weather appears to have been quite mild. Temperature records at

Fort Laramie record the afternoon high on 5 February at 48°F (9°C) (pers. comm. Jodi Preston, Wyoming Water Resources, 23 March 2006). In his recollective letter written in 1906, George Bent recalled "There was no snow on the ground although it was February. Winter of 1865 was open winter." (Haack nd, 34).

As a result of these actions, the Army force at Mud Springs grew from nine to some well-armed 140 troopers and over 200 by the evening of 7 February

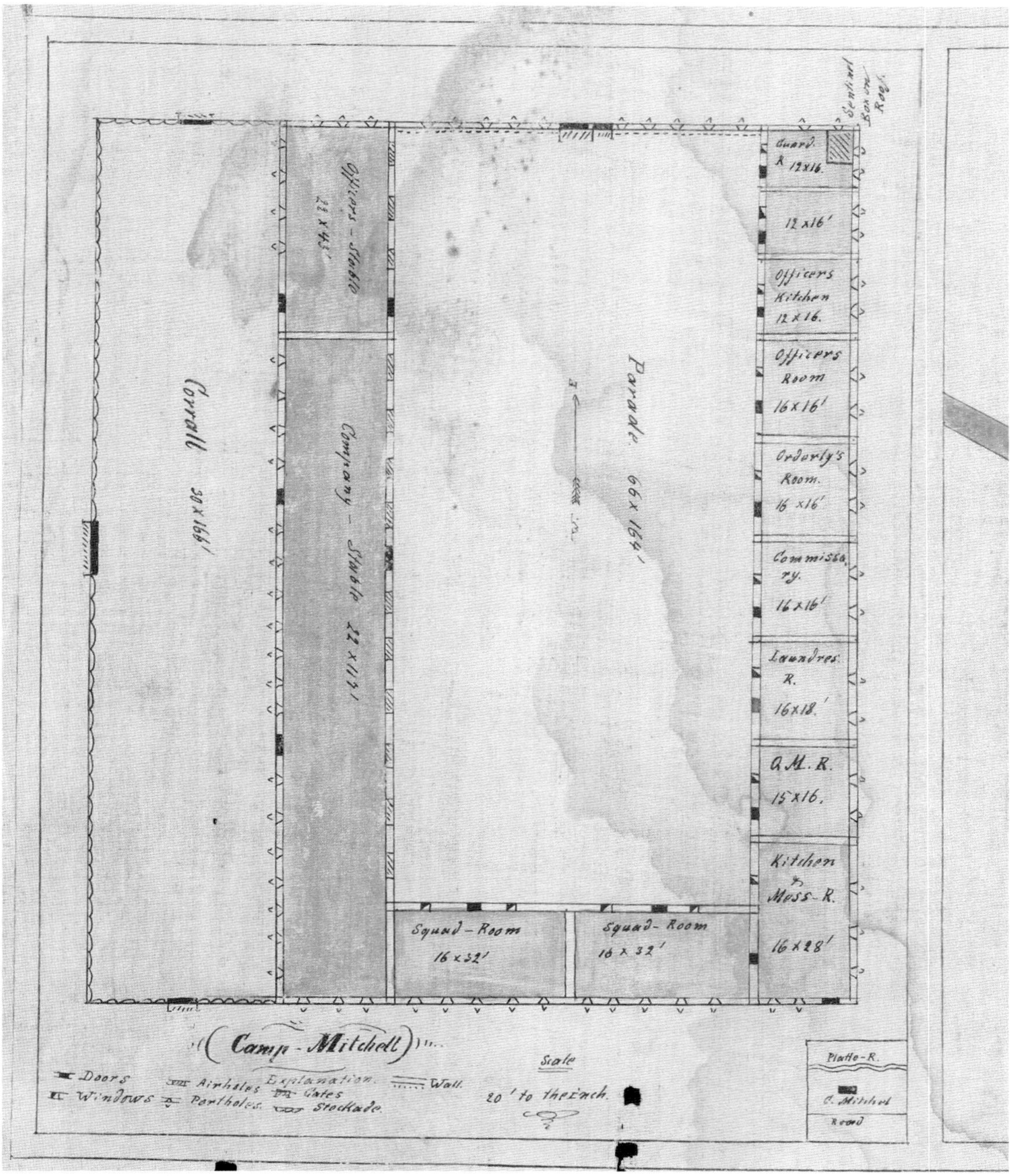

Fig. 5.5 Camp (or Fort) Mitchell: plan by Lt Caspar Collins of where part of the Mud Springs relief column originated (courtesy Colorado State University Library Archives, 10212/37595)

The Volunteer Cavalry units

11th Ohio Volunteer Cavalry (Dyer 1994, 1479; Robrock 1983)

The first four companies of the regiment were raised by Lt Col. William Oliver Collins as the 7th Ohio Volunteer Cavalry (OVC). They were to be consolidated into the 6th OVC at Camp Dennison, but Collins refused to redesignate his companies, resulting in a political dispute. The issue was settled by the Ohio Governor by creating the First Independent Battalion of Ohio Cavalry and it detaching from the 6th OVC in February 1862. Collins battalion was ordered to St Louis, Missouri, and during the month of May marched to Fort Laramie in Idaho Territory. The battalion was assigned to protect travelers and interests along the North Platte and Sweetwater Rivers, and then at South Pass, Idaho Territory, to guard the Overland Mail routes from Julesburg, Colorado, to Green River, Wyoming.

In June 1863 Collins recruited four additional companies at Camp Dennison, including 40 former Confederates enlisted from the prisoner of war camp at Camp Chase, who were to be sent west to combine, in July, with the First Independent Battalion as the 11th OVC. The additional four companies were activated as a defense against Morgan's Raid in Ohio in July before being sent to Fort Leavenworth, Kansas, at the start of August. Following the burning of Lawrence, Kansas, the battalion was sent after William Quantrill for a short time. Companies E through H arrived at Fort Laramie on 13 October 1863. Three more companies (I, K and L) were formed in 1864 from surplus recruits and men of Companies A through D who did not be re-enlist at the expiration of their enlistments.

The 11th OVC was assigned to the Department of Kansas (Department of the Missouri after 30 January 1865), District of Nebraska. Upon arrival at Fort Laramie the troops were assigned to various posts along the Sweetwater and North Platte rivers between Nebraska and South Pass. A company was sent immediately to construct Fort Halleck near Elk Mountain on the Overland Trail. Troops also manned Fort Halleck and several outlying satellite posts until they were abandoned in 1866. In 1864 two companies were sent to Camp Collins (named for Lt Col. Collins) and later Fort Collins until it too was decommissioned in 1866. Collins became commander of the West Sub-District, District of Nebraska, with his headquarters at Fort Laramie. Collins son, Caspar, served as a Lieutenant and was killed at Platte River Bridge on 26 July 1865. Caspar, Wyoming is named for him.

Companies A through D mustered out 1 April 1865, along with Collins. He was replaced in command by Lt Col. Thomas L. Mackey, former captain of Company C. Members of Companies E and K, both units of "Galvanized Yankees", accompanied the column of Brigadier General Patrick Edward Connor on the 1865 Powder River Expedition and saw action in the Battle of the Tongue River. The remaining seven companies mustered out 14 July 1866. They were the last volunteer troops from Ohio in service.

The regiment was engaged in at least 21 battles and skirmishes. Elements of the regiment fought Confederates in Indian Territory (Oklahoma) and against Native Americans on the Great Plains. Some of those fights were at Deer Creek Station, Sweetwater Station, Dry Creek, and Platte River Bridge, Sage Creek,Wyoming; and at Mud Springs and Rush Creek, Nebraska.

The 11th OVC suffered three officers and 20 enlisted men killed in action, and one officer and 60 enlisted men died from disease.

7th Iowa Volunteer Cavalry (Dyer 1994, 1162–3)

The 7th Iowa Volunteer Cavalry (IVC) was organized under authority of the War Department for the purpose of assisting in the defense of the western and northern frontier settlements against the Native American groups hostile to the United States. The organization of the regiment proceeded slowly. The first company was ordered into quarters by the Governor on 5 November 1862. Davenport, Iowa was designated as the rendezvous of the regiment and there, on dates ranging between 27 April and 13 July 1863, eight companies – A to H – were mustered into Federal service of the United States. Company I was added, by transfer of the Sioux City Cavalry (an independent company), which had been mustered into the service at Sioux City, 14 November 1861. Companies K, L and M were transferred from the 41st Iowa Battalion. The last four companies had been in service on the frontier at Fort Randall, Dakota Territory. The organization of the regiment was completed on 25 July 1863.

On July 27, 1863, six companies of the regiment, under command of Major H. H. Heath, marched from Davenport to Omaha, Nebraska, Headquarters of the District of Nebraska, Department of Missouri. Upon arrival at Omaha the companies were assigned to different posts in Nebraska Territory. On the 5 September the remaining companies marched to Omaha, where the headquarters of the regiment were established. The companies were assigned to their various posts, where they escorted trains, protected emigrants, guarded lines of travel, scouted through the country and watched the movements of the Indians. The 7th engaged in numerous fights with the Indians. Portions of the regiment were engaged in the battles of Horse Creek, Wyoming; White Stone Hill, Tahkahokutah, and Bad Lands, South Dakota; Julesburg, Colorado; and Mud Springs and Rush Creek, Nebraska, as well as several other minor skirmishes. The regiment was mustered out on 22 June 1866. In addition to official accounts, the actions and adventures of the 7th Iowa were graphically presented by Eugene F. Ware who and enlisted in 1861 and was mustered out in 1866 as Captain of Company F. After the War, he wrote poetry under the pen name Ironquill, but his 1908 volume, *The Indian Campaign of 1864*, is a major account of cavalry life along the Overland Trail.

The 7th IVC had, at the completion of its organization, an aggregate strength of 1096 men. Subsequent enlistments increased the number to the total enrollment to 1592. A total of 30 were killed in action or died of wounds received, another 18 were wounded in combat, and 93 died of disease during their service.

(see above). Collins estimated that between 500 and 1000 Indian fighters were involved in the attack. Based on estimates by other observers, McDermott (2003, 38) believes the higher number is the most accurate. The newly arrived Army troops established another corral of wagons and other materials adjacent to the station as well as, presumably, erecting tents and establishing fireplaces. They kept their stock in this confine and used it as a defensive line after 5 February. Special Order 2, issued at Mud Springs and dated 6 February 1865 is the order pertaining to that defense. It appointed Lt Harriman as adjutant and Sgt Reed as Sergeant Major of the command. The second order also required the men to keep their arms in good condition and to not waste ammunition with “inefficient firing”. It also required the command’s mounts to be “kept within the camp and carefully fastened unless in use”. Other items in the orders state that each squadron will take a place as quarters and each location was to be fortified as well as possible, and that all men and equipment for each squadron will be kept together in the respective quarters’ area.

Finally the order designated the west room of the north building as a hospital and the east room as the command headquarters and telegraph office. This statement seems to confirm that the western building was the domestic building and the eastern one the stable. Likewise what is, in fact, the north room in the west building was the telegraph office, as noted on the Collins map (Fig. 5.1) and the south room labeled as "squad room" was likely the one used as the hospital. The building orientation discrepancy between the Collins map and the description in Special Order 2 suggests a lack of clear understanding of the cardinal directions.

Three enlisted men accounts exist in the form of recollections published in the Civil War veteran newspaper the *National Tribune*. These accounts contained more information on the fight that took place a couple of days later at Rush Creek, including a fourth account on Rush Creek alone by E. M. Drake, but they also present specific details and add texture to the combat activities that took place at Mud Springs. Each man gives a similar account of the fight at Mud Springs, but they differ slightly in details, not an uncommon scenario with men recalling events more than 30 years in the past, as well as the limitations of their own ability to observe an entire event. A fifth enlisted man, A. G. Shaw was interviewed by Judge Eli Ricker in 1907, but this account, also with the benefit of 42 years of hindsight and dimming memory, is not well known, and only recently published. Complete transcriptions of the recollections are reproduced in Appendix 1.

George Rowan, formerly of Co. D, 7th IVC disputed the E. M. Drake account in his submission to the *National Tribune* published on 30 January 1890. In it he, among many "corrections", stated:

> "Although Col. Collins was a good man, yet as a soldier and an officer he was a mere cipher with shoulder-straps. Twenty-five years is a long time to remember dates and numbers, consequently Comrade Drake is excusable for his errors. I think my impartial statement, though perhaps not absolutely correct, yet more accurate and impartial than Mr. Drake's, because he barely mentions the 7th Iowa Cav., and scoops the honors for Col. Collins and the 11th Ohio Cav., both of whom cut the smallest figure in the fight, and, worst of all, wholly ignores the brave Lieutenant of his own regiment, above referred to, and whose name, I am sorry to say I have forgotten."

George Nelson, Co. I, 11th OVC attempted to correct what he perceived as errors in both the Drake and Rowan accounts in a *National Tribune* article of 1 May 1890. Nelson indicates he kept a diary during the period and used it to refresh his memory in order to offer his account of the fights at Mud Springs and Rush Creek. In reference to Rush Creek, Nelson states:

> "Feb. 4, 1865, the commander of the Post at Fort Laramie received a dispatch from Mud Springs, 110 miles distant, to the effect that the station was surrounded by a large number of Indians, and that unless speedily succored the 14 men at that place (five civilians and nine soldiers) would be killed or captured. Col. Collins, of the 11th Ohio Cav., realizing the importance of prompt action, started about dark same day to the rescue. The command consisted of parts of four companies of the 11th Ohio Cav., about 100 men,

> and Co. D, 7th Iowa Cav., about 50 men, in all about 150 men, well mounted and armed in most part with Spencer rifles and carbines. It will be seen by the above that the 11th Ohio Cav. furnished a pretty strong 'Corporal's guard'.
>
> We marched all the night of the 4th and until about 11 o'clock of the 5th, when we arrived at Fort Mitchell, one-half the distance to Mud Springs. Here we rested and refreshed ourselves and horses until about 7 p.m. when we resumed our march, the Iowa company under Capt. Foutz [*sic*] having been sent on in advance. Marching all the night of the 5th we arrived at Mud Springs about 7 o'clock on the morning of the 6th, which is the date of the Mud Springs fight, and not the 5th, as stated by Comrade Drake, nor as late as the 25th, as stated by Comrade Rowan. Meantime the 11 men in the station, which consisted of two small log houses used for telegraph office and stable, reinforced by the Iowa company, who by the way were splendid fighters, had made it so hot for Mr. 'Lo' that they had made but little headway toward reducing the station. Having marched for two nights and a day in terribly cold weather, with no sleep and but little rest, we were in rather a sorry plight, many of the men having their hands and feet badly frozen.
>
> Hastily forming a corral out of our few wagons, and thus securing our stock, we prepared to give them a warm reception, and they came at us in fine Indian fashion. Soon after the fight began Col. Collins telegraphed to Laramie for reinforcements. The 'affair' continued without intermission from 7 a.m. till dark. Our loss was very light compared with that of the Indians, as we did most of our fighting from the two log houses mentioned, while they were in the open. The Indians made several desperate attempts during the day to stampede our horses and mules and get them out of the corral. Many of their 'braves' bit the dust, or rather the sand, in these attempts, and brought them within close range of our unerring Spencers. We could not ascertain with any degree of accuracy how many warriors were killed, as most of them were tied to their ponies, a custom they have to prevent their killed from falling into the hands of their enemies. The fight ended at dark by the Indians drawing off. We rested on our arms during that night and the day of the 7th, not, however, relaxing our vigilance."

Another 11th OVC man who wrote in the *National Tribune* was David Peck of Company H. His piece was published on 10 March 1898. Peck discusses the Mud Springs fight at length:

> "Editor National Tribune: Our company (H, 11th Ohio Cav.) built Fort Mitchell, and while stationed there we received telegraphic notice that a small outpost called Mud Springs had been attacked by the savages, and asked for help. This was about 4 o'clock p.m. 'Boots and saddles' was sounded by the buglers, and every man who could be spared was soon in the saddle, and on the way to Mud Springs. The post was situated at the foot of small bluffs on one side and a small valley on the other.

> We arrived about 2 o'clock a.m.; the company halted and the bugler was ordered to sound the bugle, so that the besieged would know that help was at hand. There were only seven soldiers and four citizens to guard and protect the post.
>
> When we got to the boys the doors were thrown open and an old soldier named Idlet [William H. Idlet, Company H, 11th OVC] cried for joy. The boys knew that it was the intention of the Indians to crawl up around the building in the night, and if a head appeared it would be sure death.
>
> At daylight 16 of us (I among the number) were sent to the bluff in the rear of the post to prevent, if possible, the Indians from getting too close. We had fired several rounds at the Indians as they had galloped from one bluff to another, when about five hundred rose up behind the creek bank and fired at us. As the fire was too heavy to withstand, the order to retire was given, and just as we turned to go two brothers (Cpl Lewis Biehn, wounded, and Pvt. Jacob Biehn, died of wounds, Company B), one standing on each side of me, were shot. I was the last one to get into the building. One of the men, who had been shot through the shoulder, soon came to and ran as fast as his legs could carry him, and I opened the door. He stepped in, fell, was picked up, and placed in a bunk and given medical attention.
>
> The other brother had been shot in the hip, the ball lodging in his groin (died of wounds at Fort Laramie on February 24, 1865). We could see the Indians jumping up, waving their scalping knives and yelling like demons.
>
> As bullets and arrows were coming against the building like hail, (Sgt.) William Hall, who had seen service in the frontier and after being discharged had enlisted again in my company, asked if there was anyone who would volunteer to go with him and bring in the wounded man. No one would go; he took off his revolver belt and hung it on a peg, as unconcerned as though he was going to his supper. Officers tried to persuade him not to go, as it was almost sure death, but he opened the door, walked quickly out to the man, and placing him on his shoulder brought him safely into the house without getting even a scratch. I think the hand of Providence was surely manifested there."

Eli Ricker's interviewed former 11th OVC trooper A. G. Shaw and took place in Valentine, Nebraska on 1 September 1907. Shaw served with the unit until mustered out at the end of the war, then he was a civilian contractor for the army for several years after the Civil War. His contract happened to place him in Montana in 1877 where he saw the Little Bighorn battlefield just a year after Custer's defeat (Jensen 2005). His assessment of the affair at Mud Springs is brief but in line with other accounts:

> "... Another incident in the history of the 11th Ohio Cavalry ... The Reg't. went first to Mud Springs (then in Idaho territory, now in Neb., he says)

> which is east of Courthouse Rock, on the trail from [Lodge] Pole Creek to the Platte, just before and in sight of the Platte. This was in January, 1865. Mud Springs had been a stage station but was now abandoned as such & was at this time a telegraph station. There were several buildings, and rooms connected or a part of the same building. The Indians got behind the hill in the rear of the buildings & would crawl to the top and shoot down into the log building. There were no windows on that side, but occasionally a bullet went through the chinking and penetrated to the inside, but nobody was hurt. The attack was begun at daybreak and kept up with irregular intervals of suspension until sundown. Ceased altogether then. The Cmdg. officer sent soldiers to the top of the hill to reconnoiter the enemy's position, and several were wounded, one belonging to Co. B. fatally."

As the various accounts show, the fighting on 6 February became quite intense. In addition to continuing to try to drive off horses and mules penned in the corral, Indians also brought groups of up to 200 individuals to the top of the hill immediately south of the station. This brought them within 75 yds (*c.* 70 m) of the station buildings and allowed them to send in volleys of bullets and arrows. To deal with those attacks, on the afternoon of 6 February Collins organized an assault by mounted and unmounted troopers on the hill south of the station. After that assault, Indians abandoned the high ground. In their place, the troopers occupied the hill and even dug a "rifle pit" on its top (McDermott 2003, 39) (see Chapter 6).

With a secure perimeter and another detachment of 50 men of the 11th OVC, who arrived from Fort Laramie with a cannon late on the 6th, the Army was able to leave the station confines. On the 7th, Collins sent out scouting parties to find the main Indian camp. Following well-worn trails, it was easily located. On the morning of the 8th, Collins led a force of troopers out of Mud Springs to pursue the Cheyenne and their allies who were, by that time, breaking their Rush Creek camp and heading across the North Platte. At that point, the battle of Mud Springs was over.

When Collins moved his command on the afternoon of the 8 February to try to intercept the Indians at their camp on Rush Creek, he left at least seven wounded men and ten men suffering from frostbite behind at Mud Springs Station, along with the now dismounted station guard and the civilians. He also detached Capt. Fouts, Co. D, 7th IVC, to protect the station and its wounded and sick. Presumably some of the 40 men accompanying Fouts stayed behind to provide the guard, along with the regimental surgeon, and perhaps some of the staff officers and enlisted personnel. It can be assumed that at least 50 men were probably left at Mud Springs while Collins's force probably consisted of 180, or fewer, men for the march to Rush Creek.

In sum, historical sources indicate that the Mud Springs battle involved more than 200 U.S. troops and upwards of 1000 Indian fighters. The two sides fought for more than 3 days, using a variety of firearms and traditional weapons. Casualties are uncertain, but seem light. Collins (Collins Report, OR) reported three men seriously and four slightly wounded at Mud Springs. No Army soldiers were killed outright in the fighting although Pvt Jacob Biehn, Co. B, 11th OVC died at Fort Laramie on 24 February of wounds received during the Mud Springs fight (11th OVC Regimental Records). Of the six other Mud Springs wounded three can be specifically identified: Cpl. Lewis Biehn (brother to Jacob), Saddler Lewis Boeschlein, and Pvt Imry Louderback, all of Company B, 11th OVC. Collins also reported ten men disabled due to frostbite acquired on the march from Forts Laramie and Mitchell. The identity of these men is uncertain, but may include: Pvt Henry Parker, Co. A, who died of pneumonia at Fort Laramie on 23 March 1865; Pvt Adam Phillips, Co. A, who died of infection resulting in amputation of his feet due to frostbite on 9 March at Fort Laramie; and Pvt George Butler, Co. L, who was discharged from the service on 20 September at Fort Laramie for loss of his toes due to frostbite (*Official Roster of the Soldiers of the State of Ohio in the War of the Rebellion, 1861–1866*).

No Indian bodies were observed although Army participants suggested that some 30 of their adversaries had been dispatched. George Bent says no Indians were killed in the fighting at Mud Springs (Hyde 1983, 193). The fight did not mark a decisive point in frontier military history, but the formal report Collins prepared on the fight appears to have been read and considered by military leaders (McDermott 2003, 35–45).

By the afternoon of 7 February fighting at Mud Springs was essentially over. For both Indian and Army fighters the strategic value and tactical potential of the station had changed dramatically. Lt Col. Collins and his troopers had secured the station but they were in an isolated location and could not be sure that travel along the overland trail was safe. For Cheyenne fighters, easily stolen horses and cattle were no longer to be had in corrals near the station. Instead a well-organized and aggressive force of more than 200 troopers had arrived. The troopers controlled the area of the station and removed the prospect for booty or valorous display. Furthermore, with an established lookout post atop the hill to the south of the station it had become very difficult – and certainly dangerous – for Cheyenne fighters to approach it unnoticed. Beyond all of that, the presence of a well-armed force – with a cannon! – less than 10 miles (16 km) from the home community at the Rush Creek camp constituted a major security threat to the Cheyenne and their allies. Both sides prepared to move on and the fighting took a new direction.

6

The archaeology of the Mud Springs battle

In the late winter and spring of 2006 a team of interdisciplinary researchers from the University of Nebraska-Lincoln (UNL) undertook a project to find and document the archaeological evidence of the fight at Mud Springs. Archaeological investigation to seek battle debris from the February 1865 battle was aimed at documenting its importance as a battle place and to understand the role the terrain or landscape played in the fighting as we have defined in the battlespace model (see Chapter 3). To do this the limits of the battlefield and the extent of the contested zone needed to be determined. The types of guns used by Indian fighters also needed clarification. We also sought to clarify the operational aspects of the fight. Descriptions of "bo-peep" exchanges and volley firing at charging mounted warriors seem graphic, but it is not clear how the local terrain was used to support those action.

Systematic metal detection provided an appropriate means of addressing these issues (see Chapter 9) since we could assume that most surviving artifacts of war are metallic. Even though the site, which is on private land, had been subject to repeated amateur metal detecting over many years, no systematic professional archaeological investigation had ever been undertaken. The UNL metal detecting effort proved successful.

The archaeological assemblage

Cartridges, cartridge cases, and bullets form the majority of the artifacts recovered at Mud Springs (Fig. 6.2, below). In total, 44 cartridges, cases and bullets in the systematically recovered assemblage dated to the period of the battle present at the site (Bleed and Scott 2008; 2009). The gun related artifacts were analyzed employing standard archaeological firearm identification methods like those developed during the Little Bighorn battle archaeological project (Scott *et al.* 1989).

Firearm identification analysis determined the bullets (Fig. 6.1) and cartridges were fired from the following weapons: 36-caliber Starr revolver, .44-caliber Henry rifle, .44-caliber Wesson carbine, .54-caliber Leman rifle,

.56-56 Spencer and Joslyn carbines, and .58-caliber rifled musket, either a rebored M1841 rifle, a M1855, M1861, M1863, or an Enfield P53 rifled musket. Additionally, a single "top hat" or "musket cap" was found during the test excavation of the rifle pit. The cap is unfired, as it bears no tool marks from being struck by a hammer (Weber and Scott 2006, 131–43).

Beyond identifying the kinds of guns used at Mud Springs, firearm identification of the archaeologically recovered materials indicates that there were at least 21 different firearms used during the 1865 Mud Springs battle. This number includes at least 1 .36-caliber Starr revolver, 1 .44-caliber Colt M1860 army revolver, 2 .44-caliber Henry rifles, 5 .44-caliber Wesson carbines, 1 .54-caliber Leman rifle, 2 56-56-caliber Joslyn carbines, 8 56-56 Spencer carbines, and 1 .58-caliber rifled musket.

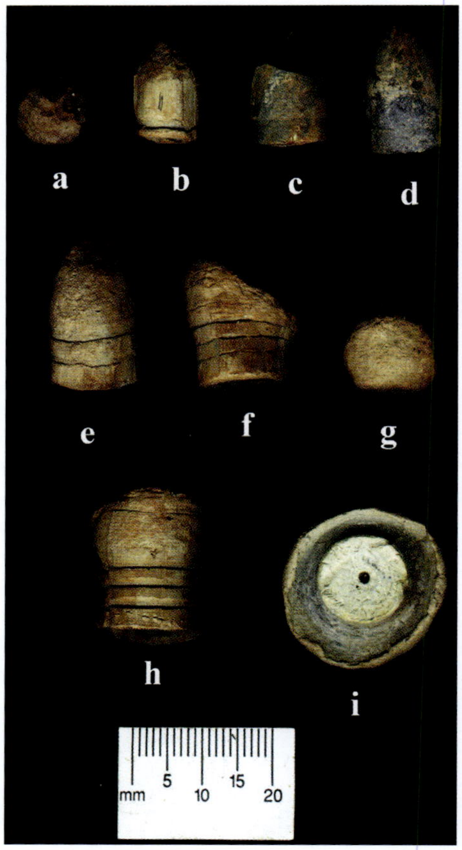

Fig. 6.1 Bullets: a) .36-caliber spherical ball (FS21); b) .36-caliber St Louis style conical bullet (FS32); c) .44-caliber bullet, unfired but with the nose altered by carving (FS5); d) .44-caliber bullet fired in a Wesson rifle (FS10); e) .50-caliber bullet fire in a 6 right land and groove barrel (FS38); f) impact deformed .50-caliber bullet fired in a 6 right land and groove barrel (FS29); g) .54-caliber spherical ball with land and groove marks, also note sprue remains at top (FS31); h) .58-caliber Minié ball (FS37); i) .50-caliber bullet mushroomed by impact and fired in a 6 right land and groove barrel, probably an 1886 Winchester (FS26) (Bleed and Scott 2009)

Firearms artifact distribution

It was no surprise that only a small number of artifacts were recovered given the land owner statements that he has allowed relic hunters on the site on a routine basis, as long as they asked permission. He recalled that previous collectors found handfuls of Spencer and other cartridge cases.

Nevertheless, the systematically archaeologically recovered cartridge cases and bullets do not appear to be randomly distributed (Fig. 6.2). Rather the find pattern distribution is consistent with the historic battle accounts. The Spencer and Joslyn cartridge cases representing eight and two separate guns respectively were found scattered around the traditional location of the Mud Spring station buildings. Cartridge cases fired from those same guns were found on the north side of the hill and on top of the hill south of the station, as well as in a low area between the south hill and a rise to the west. This distribution is consistent with the Army accounts of the battle, with the soldiers fortifying the station even after arrival of the relief columns. The Spencer and Joslyn cartridge cases found around the south hill and to the west are also consistent with Lt Col. Collins's report (Collins Report, OR) of making a mounted sortie to the south and driving the attacking warriors from the hill and the general area.

The .44-caliber Wesson cartridge cases, representing five guns, and the .44-caliber Henry cartridge cases, representing two guns, were recovered either on the rise or ridge to the southwest of the station buildings or behind a low rise on the lower west flank of the south hill. This distribution along with that of the bullets is consistent with not only warrior utilized positions but Collins attack on the warrior positions.

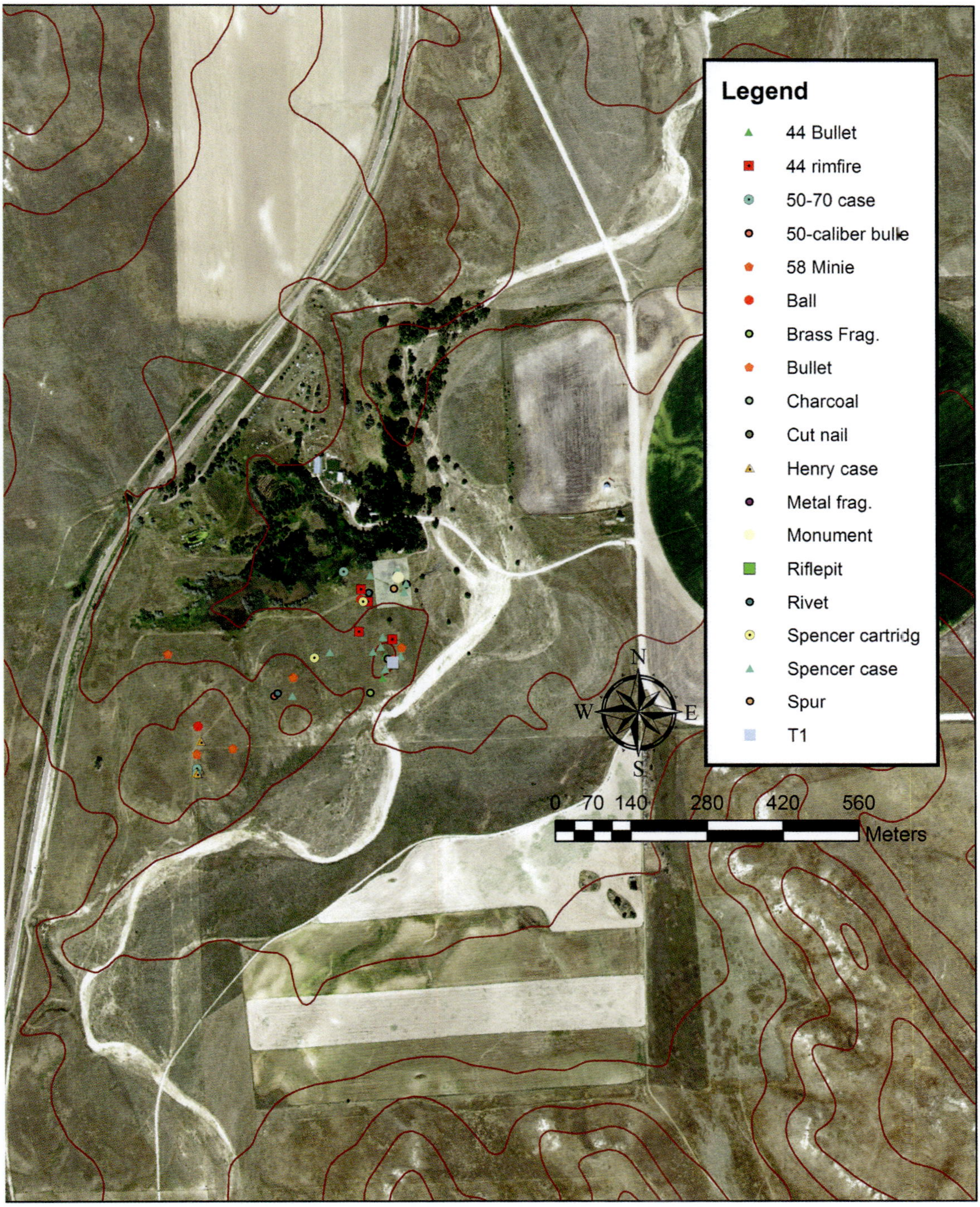

Fig. 6.2 Distribution of artifacts found at Mud Springs Station site during the metal detector inventory (authors' image)

Aside from systematic metal detecting two other geophysical methods were also employed with the intent of determining if remains of the Mud Springs station buildings have an archaeological expression (Bleed *et al.* 2014) based on previous geophysical investigations (Steinacher 1995). Ten complete and

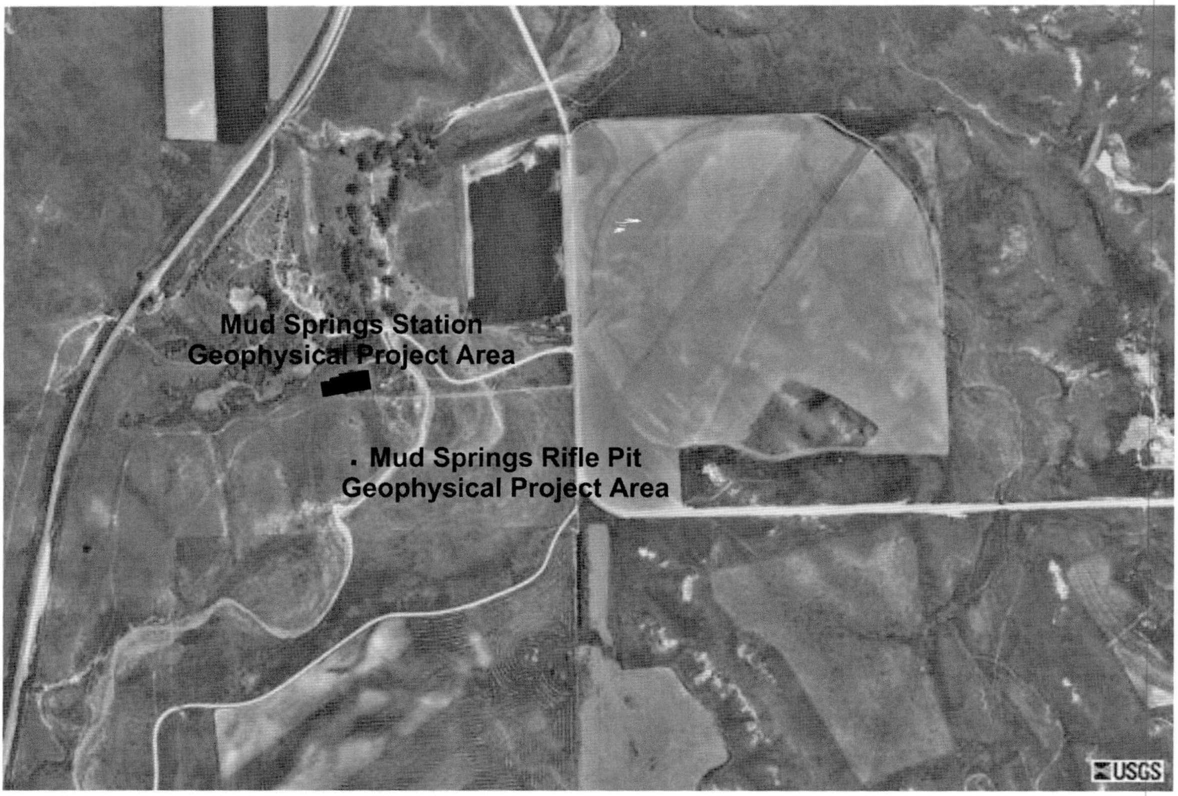

Fig. 6.3 Location of geophysical grids at the Mud Springs site (image source?)

partial 20m by 20m grid units were established for a geophysical project area measuring 3700 m^2 or 0.91 acres (Fig. 6.3). A fluxgate magnetometer was used to collect data in the grids. After processing the data, a rectangular area of magnetic anomalies in the vicinity of the potential locations of one of the two structures at the Mud Springs Station was noted (Figs 6.4 and 6.5).

Ground penetrating radar (GPR) survey of the Mud Springs geophysical project area was also conducted. A rectangular area is present in the GPR data in the same locations as the concentration of magnetic anomalies. The rectangular area is interpreted as the foundation to one of the Mud Spring Station structures. The combined findings of the magnetometry and GPR surveys strengthen the conclusion that we were able to relocate buildings associated with the Pony Express station and road ranch (Fig. 6.6). It appears the most western building, the telegrapher's office, is the one most visible in the geophysical data. The eastern building likely is obscured by the iron in the Pony Express monument and associated disturbance related to the placement of the monuments and fence.

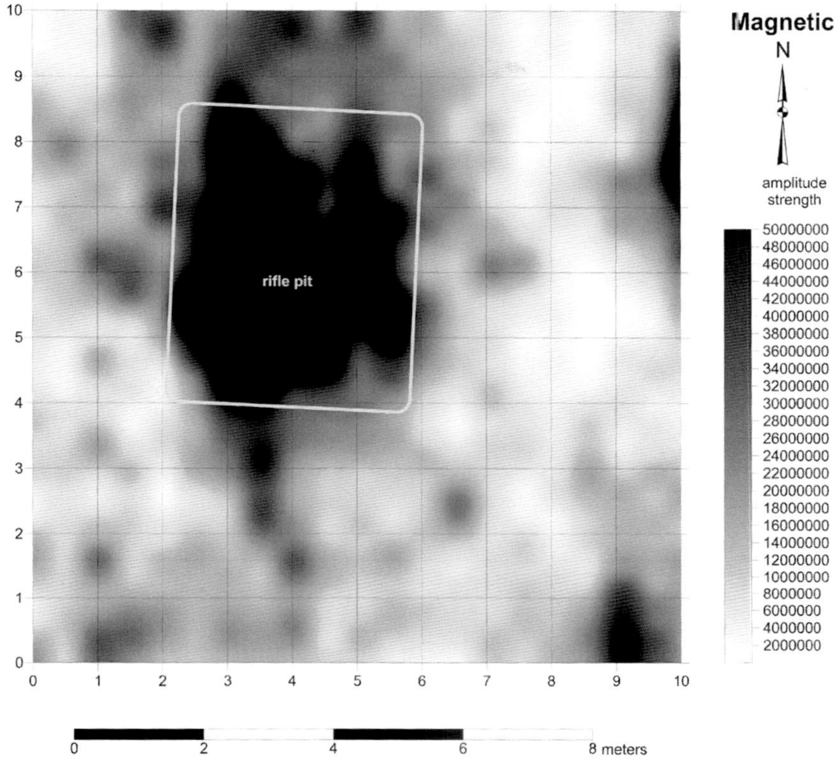

Fig. 6.4 Magnetic signature of one of the Mud Springs Station structures (courtesy Steven De Vore, Midwest Archeological Center, National Park Service, image in public domain)

Fig. 6.5 (below) Interpretation of the magnetic data that suggests the location of one of the Mud Springs structures is archaeologically intact, although the other has suffered from various modern disturbances (courtesy Steven De Vore, Midwest Archeological Center, National Park Service, image in public domain)

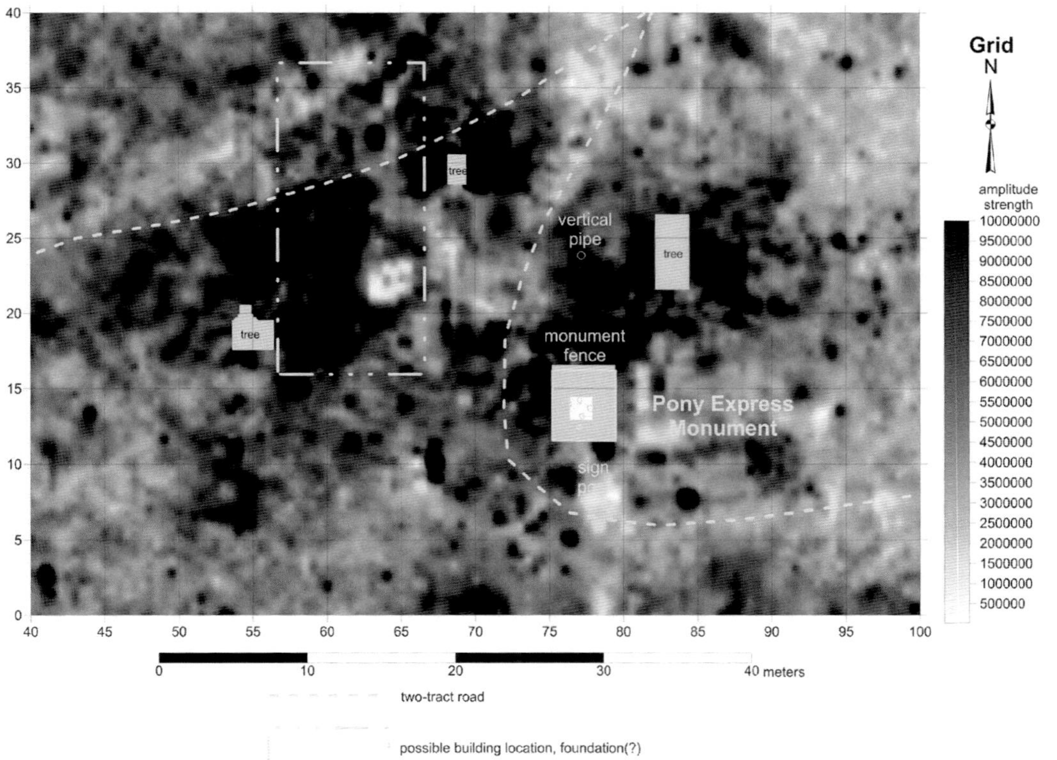

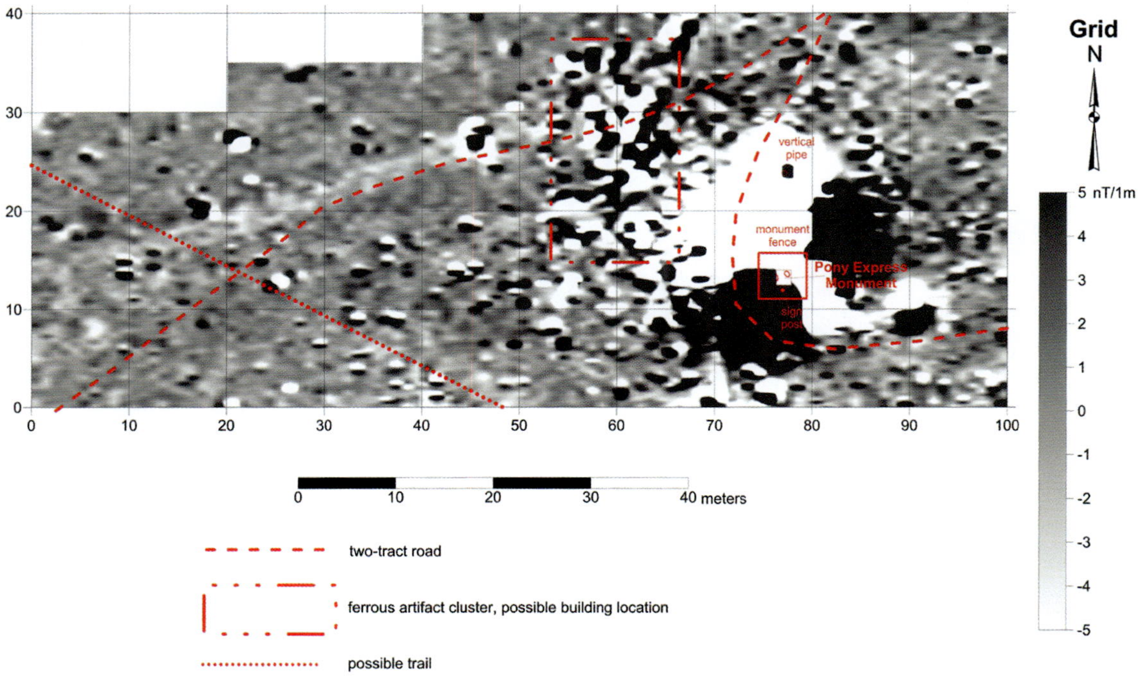

Fig. 6.6 Combining all of the geophysical data provides a picture of the Mud Springs site, suggesting some trail elements, the rifle pit and at least one structure have good archaeological signatures (courtesy Steven De Vore, Midwest Archeological Center, National Park Service, image in public domain)

The "rifle pit" feature

Given the mention that Collins's troops dug a rifle pit after they arrived at Mud Springs, a depression observed on the top of the hill south of the Mud Springs Station deserved specific investigation and documentation as an important landscape feature. Expedient defenses have a long military history. They were used in Civil War engagements (Beck 2013, 92), but they are presumed to be less common in western fights. Surviving examples of Civil War era rifle pits are quite rare.

There are a number of "blow outs" that interrupt the sod on the hilltop. An early Mud Springs battle researcher, Henderson (1951), mentioned observing multiple "pits" in his early history of the battle. He may have confused a number of natural wind caused depressions, known as "blow outs" with locations he believed to be rifle pits. However, a careful study of the hilltop showed only one of the interruptions to be consistent with a consciously excavated feature. There is some oral history associated with this feature that appears to conflict with the assumption that it is the pit Collins reports (Collins Report, OR) to have excavated during the fighting at Mud Springs. That is one reason that the team decided to conduct geophysical investigations as well as a test excavation on the feature – to determine its origin and function.

The observed depression was roughly circular, approximately 2 m in diameter and about 20 cm lower than the surrounding ground level. A test unit opened to assess the depression was laid out across what appeared to be the western margin of the original pit (Fig. 6.7). The profile of the south

Fig. 6.7 A small test pit was placed across the depression possibly identified as a rifle pit. Geophysical investigation as well as the archaeological testing confirm the location as a rifle pit (authors' image)

wall/section of the text unit, however, did not reveal a clear excavated edge. Below the thin layer of matted vegetation, the pit fill consisted of mixed gray sand that contained charcoal flecks and artifacts including the mid-portion of a bifacially flaked lithic projectile point and four flake fragments, and an unused percussion cap. There was no apparent edge to this level that might reflect the excavated edge of a rifle pit, but it was thickest toward the center of the depression. Below the gray sand layer the soil consisted of more solidly compacted sandy loam. The divide between this layer and the mixed sand was distinct enough to potentially reflect an artificial surface. No artifacts were found below this level. The top of the undisturbed sandy loam seems to form a gentle depression that at its deepest point is some 60 cm below the current soil surface. Test excavation of the potential rifle pit indicates that it is a shallow artificial feature that was excavated to have sloping sides.

Geophysical investigation (Bleed *et al.* 2014) of the suspected rifle pit employing GPR identified a small shallow rectilinear anomaly consistent with known rifle pit construction in the same area as the depression. A third technique was employed to further evaluate the rifle pit theory.

The feature was also subjected to a viewshed analysis in Geographic Information Systems (GIS) software. This has become a refined archaeological tool (Wheatley and Gillings 2002) that can expose settlement choices (Jones 2006) and visual landscapes (Llobera 2007). In military parlance this is known as terrain analysis or weapons fan analysis.

Weapons fan analysis is military amplification of viewshed methodology. If a viewshed defines those areas of a landscape visible from a given point, weapons fan analysis combines the viewshed approach with technical information of the weaponry in actual use to determine potential targets to be had from a military emplacement. Weapons fan analysis builds easily on firearms analysis since it makes use of the same kinds of ballistic information. The Mud Spring rifle pit calculated viewshed was based on the functional range of the firearms available at the time.

The analysis involved the consideration of the rifle pit's location within the context of a computerized Digital Elevation Model (DEM). The DEM contains elevation data for the area surrounding Mud Springs Station, and allows the calculation of the precise land area which was visible from any given point around the station, known as a point's viewshed. When known effective weapon range data were also incorporated, the GIS analysis allowed the effectiveness of different combat positions to be assessed, providing information on both visible land area and targets which would actually be within range of the observer's weapon. In general, an observer near the buildings of the station would have had good all-round visibility of the land near the structures, but long-distance observation to the south, east and west was obscured by rolling hills, including the south-west hill rising only 100 yds (*c.* 90 m) from the station.

Conversely, an observer from the rifle pit atop the hill had a significant advantage in visibility, being able to take advantage of long-distance views to the north, east and south, and maintaining moderate visibility to the west (Fig. 6.8). The weapons fan analysis, presenting the selection of targets which would have been available to an observer at each position, also indicated an advantage for the rifle pit on the hill, but not nearly as dramatic. Though some targets would have been available to a soldier in the pit which would not have been to a man in the station, the rifle pit position also included a number of blind spots which would have allowed opponents to approach within 20 m (25 ft) of the pit without the soldiers in the position being able to retaliate. For these reasons, the GIS analysis indicated that the rifle pit was intended primarily as an observation point to ascertain the movements and detect the approach of potential attackers, rather than as a defensive position in its own right (Bleed and Scott 2008; 2009).

Interpreting the actions and evidence of Mud Springs

The archaeological assemblage indicates that the two sides that met at Mud Springs were surprisingly well-matched. Indian fighters appear to have had a wider array of arms than U.S. troops, but the armaments of the two sides seem fully comparable. The fighting left material signatures that suggest, however, that the two sides were tactically different. The artifact distribution across the landscape indicates that the warriors used the available terrain to their advantage during the fight. They fired at the station from behind the crest of the south hill (Fig. 6.9), from behind a small rise on its lower flanks, and from behind a rise to the west. All locations were well within range of the warrior firearms and return fire from the soldiers and civilians in the station.

KOCOA (Key Terrain, Obstacles, Cover and Concealment, Observation and Fields of Fire, and Avenues of Approach)

The landscape analysis was informed by the KOCOA process. KOCOA is an acronym, adapted from military training manuals, for identifying key aspects of battlefield terrain (Babits 2013, 263–70). The original intent as stated in United States Army Field Manuals (US Army 2001; 1986) is to inform commanders and junior leaders about their area of concern in order for them to make informed decisions on their courses of action in battle (Babits 2013; McNutt 2014). The military teach battlespace concepts as part of large level command and control decision making and the KOCOA model at the most basic unit levels, squad and platoon of small unit tactics. KOCOA analysis is actually one subset of three military formats that both guide and explain battlefield activity and are presented as small unit leadership. Together with the principles of war, these frameworks provide a key for understanding behavior during battle. The Levels of War model has multiple components to include: Strategy, Tactics, Operations, and Logistics, then KOCOA, and finally, the Principles of War. Archaeologists have employed these concepts to inform their findings in conflict and battlefield sites. Essentially archaeologists use the concepts in a reverse manner to the military as a means to either find the sites of conflict as a predictive model (McMutt 2014) or as an analytical tool to aid in the interpretation of why a conflict site is in a certain place or explain the outcome of a battle in terms of a landscape theme or analytical process.

KOCOA has five key factors that aid in explaining a military unit's terrain and the potential or actual use of that terrain. The elements are defined as:

Key Terrain depends on the mission. It is any land form or localized area that provides an advantage if held by one side or the other.

Obstacles, both natural and manmade, restrict terrain use by creating problems for an advance, withdrawal, or the movement of support elements.

Cover and Concealment are different. Cover is protection from enemy fire. Concealment is protection from enemy observation.

Observation and Fields of Fire are inter-related. The first is viewscape, defined as what can be seen from a position. Fields of fire relates to both sides' weapons capabilities, including direct and indirect fire.

Avenues of Approach are the routes by which a force can attack a defensive position. Cover and concealment must be considered so as to protect attackers and allow no dead space to interfere with a defense.

Recovered ammunition is consistent with intense fire from near the station. Volley fire at mounted fighters and shots by mounted raiders, which are described in historical accounts of the fight, are not readily apparent even though hills and surfaces well removed from the station were surveyed. Archaeologically, the margins of the Mud Spring Battle were very hard to recognize. In part this may be due to indiscriminant relic collecting over the

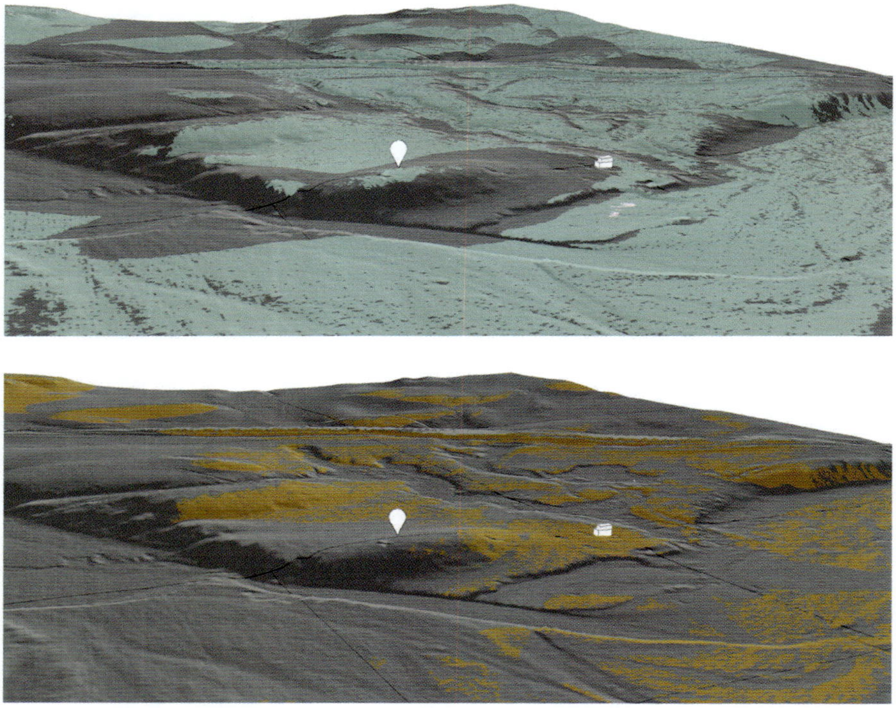

Fig. 6.8 Modelled viewshed of the terrain that could be seen by a person occupying the rifle pit. The viewshed demonstrates good views to the south and east in particular. Cheyenne warriors would have approached Mud Springs Station from those directions (authors' original reconstruction)

years. The area of dry creek to the east of the station may have changed due to flooding and other fluvial events. However, the rifle pit excavated to the south of the station seems to have altered the fight and essentially changed the Mud Spring battlespace.

A weapons fan analysis, a form of KOCOA analysis in area of cover and concealment as well as observation, shows what views of the surrounding landscape would have been available to soldiers or stockmen in the Mud Springs Station or for a picket stationed at the rifle pit on the hill to the south. The calculated weapons fans show clearly, that gunmen could see and cover most areas around the station. There were two exceptions. The hill to the south of the station hid much of that area so that Cheyenne warrior attackers could approach unseen to within 100 m (*c* 110 yds) of the station (Fig. 6.10). The far horizons were both out of rifle range and not visible from the station. The archaeological evidence shows that warriors used that landscape to fire on the occupants of the Mud Springs station complex minimizing their exposure to hostile fire from the soldiers._

Long distance viewsheds, KOCOA key terrain, observation, and avenues of approach, document that most of the areas visible from the station, together with distant vistas, were visible for a 1.5 m (5 ft) tall individual standing at the tested rifle pit. The hill top rifle pit allowed a view of the distant plains to the south and west. An individual stationed in the rifle pit, whether sitting to reduce his profile to the biting winds that blow across it in February or standing to

Fig. 6.9 A modern photograph taken from the military crest of the hill south of Mud Springs Station shows the view of the station site that would have been seen by the Cheyenne warriors occupying the hill (authors' image)

Fig. 6.10 A modern photograph taken from the station site looking south toward the hill occupied by the Cheyenne. From this view it is obvious those occupying the station could see little of their attackers' approach (authors' image)

increase his overall view area, could easily see the areas to the north, south and east giving effective warning time for the defenders to anyone approaching from those directions. The location especially afforded a good view of the territory to the east that was crossed by riders traveling back and forth between Mud Springs and the Rush Creek camp. Areas to the north, southeast and immediately west of the station were visible enough to give the defenders effective warning time for anyone approaching from those directions.

Clearly, the pit would have been a good lookout post. But since soldiers could see farther than they could shoot, the weapons fan from the pit is very different from its distant viewshed. The hilltop weapons fan reached a few areas that could not be hit from the station, but it was far less than perfect. It was certainly fragmented, so that warriors could approach from the west unseen to within 20 m (65 ft) of the pit should they have not been detected at longer distances. Beyond that, the hill to the southwest of the station covered an area big enough to serve as a staging area for mounted raids. The pit was, thus, not well placed for combative defense of the soldiers' position. If the rifle pit was occupied by soldiers after breaking the station siege, other pickets or guards must have covered the western approaches. If the pit was occupied in order to provide a view of attackers coming from the south, it was an effective location that allowed for ample time to warn those camped around or in the station of on-coming warrior groups.

The archaeological remains from the Mud Springs battle site are not plentiful but a combination of documentary evidence, non-invasive survey techniques, metal detecting and very small scale excavation has allowed us not only to make considerable sense of the physical space of the battle, and to corroborate the eye-witness accounts (at least to some extent), but also to consider the strategy of the combatants and the wider battlespace of the conflict.

7

The road to Rush Creek

By the evening of 7 February the military situation in the North Platte seems to have been quiet but it was far from stable. Both Indian and Army fighters could find tactical success in the fighting that had taken place at Mud Springs. Cheyenne and allied fighters had engaged enemy forces. They had captured horses and cattle and engaged in public acts of bravery that would certainly carry social benefits (see Chapter 4). Army forces had acted well. They had promptly come to the aid of a unit in need and easily gained control of the Station that had been attacked. Still, the strategic situation for both sides was far less than secure. Lt Col. Collins and his troopers had secured Mud Springs and gotten themselves rested and organized, but they were in an isolated location and could not assure safe travel along the overland trail. For Cheyenne fighters, easily stolen horses and cattle were no longer to be had in corrals near the station. Instead, a well-organized and aggressive force of more than 200 troopers was crowded around what had been a small post. This force absolutely controlled the area of the station and reduced the prospect for booty or gallant display. Furthermore, with an established lookout post atop the hill to the south of the Station it had become very difficult – and certainly dangerous – for Indian fighters to approach unnoticed. The fighting had to take a new direction and both sides had to move on.

The movements that marked the next phase of the North Platte fighting are easy to understand in general terms. Both sides were set up for mobile action so movement would have been practised and well within their capabilities. Their movements after Mud Springs are also generally documented in historical sources and easy to understand in strategic and operational terms. Nevertheless, movements that followed Mud Springs and led to the next battle are not known in specific detail. The routes that the competing forces followed, the ways they reacted to terrain features, and how the landscape they crossed influenced the combat that resulted are not known in specific detail. This chapter aims to combine historical sources and modern geospatial techniques, landscape insights, and precious few archaeological traces to describe the movement of Army and Cheyenne forces that led up to the next major confrontation that occurred near the mouth of Rush Creek on 8 and 9 February 1865.

Cheyenne movements away from the camp on Rush Creek

Rush Creek is the original name of a spring fed stream that flows, continually, from its source in the rocky bluffs that form the south side of the North Platte valley. From it source to its meeting at the North Platte the creek crosses only about 6 miles (*c.* 10 km). It is rarely more than a few feet wide, but it flows continuously with fresh water. The Cheyenne community that moved into the North Platte valley established their camp near the head waters of the Creek. With some 2000 people, their gear, recently acquired booty including a herd of more than 1000 captured cattle and many wagons, this settlement probably spread across a large area.

As a dependable source of water in a sheltered location, the head of Rush Creek would have been perennially attractive. Unfortunately, very little archaeological evidence of the Rush Creek camp survives. Today it has become a large farmstead and, for some years, the spring water supported a large, productive fish hatchery. With those uses the area has been much altered.

Fig. 7.1 GIS derived least cost path (black) and possible movement corridors (grey) between Mud Springs station and the Cheyenne Rush Creek headwaters campsite superimposed on digital elevation model emphasizing the terrain features that had to be negotiated. With insights from scouts and outriders, the cavalry could have moved rather freely across this zone (authors' original reconstruction)

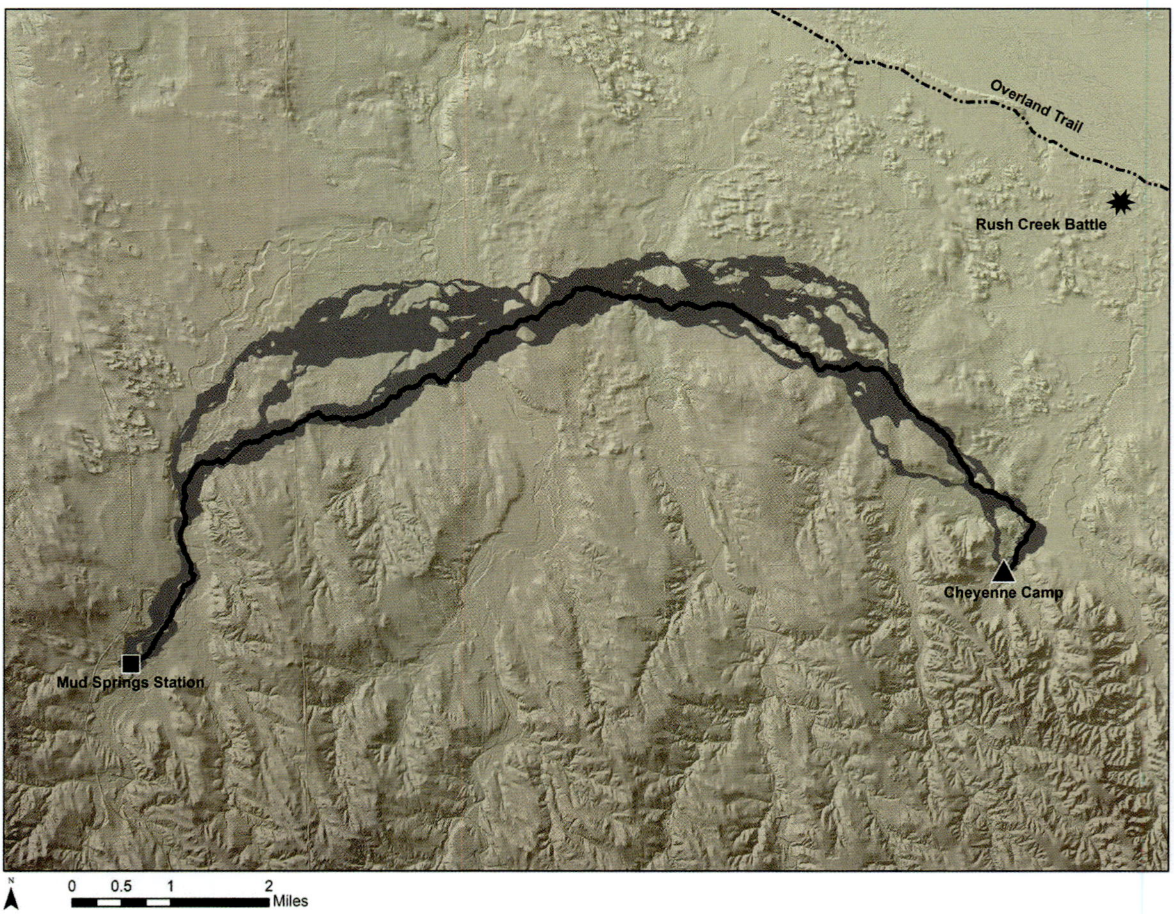

However, much of the area is still littered with lithic debris that has to indicate that it has had a long history of use by Native folks. We can only assume that the Cheyenne and Lakota travelers who established their home on the site on 3 February 1865 were dropping by a familiar stopping place.

Battlespace terminology is easily applied to the military situation faced by the Cheyenne and their allies. The Rush Creek camp was serving as a home station since it was a place where non-combatants could find shelter for themselves and their stock. Almost incidentally, the Rush Creek camp also provided a force projection base from which warriors could foray out against the Mud Springs Station. Using the high land to the east of the telegraph station, mounted fighters could safely move toward the station. As skilled riders with many new mounts, the Indian fighter probably found the 8 mile (13 km) trip between Mud Springs and where their families were comfortably ensconced a very manageable commute (Fig. 7.1). The Cheyenne also certainly understood trail routes and the local terrain around the Rush Creek camp and knew how to use it to provide food and shelter. They had a broad area of interest and they knew how to employ their knowledge of their general surroundings. Beyond that area of interest, Indian fighters could also easily obtain intelligence information regarding the whereabouts and activities of U.S. Army troops. It seems fair to assume that the Indian forces comfortably controlled the battlespace surrounding the Rush Creek camp.

As fighting at Mud Springs was resolved and the strategic situation changed, the Indian community moved on from their Rush Creek base. This community move appears to have started on 7 February. It may have been somewhat rushed, but it was basically a continuation of an already established trek into the Sand Hills where they would be securely isolated from troopers who rarely left the trails. Information on the move was gathered from Cheyenne veterans interviewed by G. B. Grinnell (1956, 189). George Bent also took part in the move and recalled it in later correspondence (McDermott 2003, 39ff). Bent's recollection was that the Indian community hastily struck their tents, assembled their gear, moved down the west side of Rush Creek and across the frozen North Platte. They passed the night of 7 February and most of 8 February in a short term camp in the bluffs north of the river, which offered protection against attacks as the area north of the river was open territory where the Army seldom ventured. The location of this camp site has not been identified, but it must have been in or near the modern community of Broadwater, Nebraska where archaeological traces are not easily found.

The army's pursuit

Lt Col. Collins led a column of cavalry out of Mud Springs on the morning of 8 February. By that time, the troops who had rushed to the Station were rested, organized and ready for further action. Injured men and those with serious frostbite were separated and left with a security detachment at Mud Springs under Capt. Fouts. The rest of the Collins's forces formed into an expeditionary column ready to find and engaged the Cheyenne community that had entered the North Platte Valley.

Collins had dispatched scouts on 7 February to locate the Cheyenne camp so he understood that his pursuit would have to be to the east and beyond the hill that hid much of the country in that direction. In his after-action report (Collins Report, OR) Collins stated that he expected the Cheyenne to be camped at the head of Rush Creek, but it is likely that that assessment was general rather than specific. The crossing where Rush Creek flows into the North Platte River was a known point on the overland trail, but it is unlikely that Collins or other army forces had ever had reason to visit the headwaters of Rush Creek. In addition to having a rather uncertain goal, Collins's objective also seems quite vague. He and his force had to be ready for action but they were proceeding with care since they did not know where their adversaries were likely to be.

Information about Collin's pursuit, with a rather detailed order of march, survive in his papers (Collins Papers, DPL). In his Special Order 3, dated 8 February 1865 at Headquarters in the Field at Mud Springs, Collins orders his squadron commanders to be ready to march without delay. The order specified that Lt Brown was to be in charge of the Mountain Howitzer, and the command would advance in pursuit of the Indians in a specific order. Collins placed the 3rd Squadron out as the advance unit with orders to keep out scouting parties to the front of the column. Second in the march order was the field piece which was to be kept masked until ready to fire. This suggests the gun and carriage were not towed by a mule or horse, but perhaps disassembled and packed for transport on mules or horses or even hidden in a wagon.

The Mountain Howitzer (Fig. 7.2) was followed by the 2nd Squadron and the 4th Squadron. Each were to send scouts out on the flanks. First Squadron was to follow in the rear and place scouts out in that direction. Collins also stated the wagon train was to immediately be corralled on proper ground if the column was attacked: 1st Squadron was likely the wagon train guard as well as the rear guard.

The column, if marching in column of twos and at regulation spacing, would be over 1000 ft long (300 m) at a minimum if there were only five wagons. It would increase to over one-quarter mile (0.4 km) long if there were ten wagons. If the column marched single file then it extended to between 2000 and 2500 ft in length (*c.* 600–750 m). If in a column of fours the length would be reduced from 1000 ft to something over 500 ft (150 m+) depending on the number of wagons. The scouts or flankers covering the front, rear and column flanks the column were likely deployed up to one quarter mile out or perhaps less. Regardless, Collins command covered a substantial area and even in February could have created a dust cloud that would have been visible for some distance.

Archaeological study of movement is an interesting but difficult topic.

Raw materials found far from their source area or goods discovered away from where they are known to have been produced are commonly treated as archaeological evidence of movement. Addressing movement itself is a more challenging task since finding material signatures of where and how mobile units moved across landscapes is difficult. Where prepared trails can be archaeologically observed (Bell and Lock 2000, 85–100), contact routes and travel networks can be either observed or inferred. When the movements were brief or exploratory and the travelers lightly equipped, attempting to trace them with the tools of archaeology may be a daunting prospect, but movement is an important part of conflict archaeology.

In order to build movement into our assessment of the North Platte campaign as battlespace we initially hoped to find archaeological evidence of Collins's advance. The route that he took when he left Mud Springs was neither recorded nor marked, but the column he led, with some 120 mounted troopers and four or five wagons, each drawn by harnessed teams, carried thousands of buckles, buttons, and small gear that was subject to loss. The volunteers from Ohio and Iowa who made up the column were experienced and proud of their abilities as "frontiersmen" (Ware 1994), but after nearly 3 years of service, their gear must have been well-worn. We hoped that there might have been sufficient lost gear to show how the column responded to the topography it met along the route. Our attempts to recognize traces of Collins's movements involved pleasant explorations of areas the column may have crossed. We also spoke with landowners to ask if they had noted gear that may have been dropped by cavalry troopers. Those efforts yielded no clear results, so we decided to approach the movement of 8 February with the analytical and predictive tools of modern Geographic Information Systems (GIS).

To determine the location of potential routes Collins's column took between Mud Springs station and the Cheyenne campsite, a corridor analysis was conducted using GIS. The analysis assesses the terrain in a particular area and identifies the challenges associated with different travel routes. Routes that offer the fewest challenges – features like creek valleys or steep hills – represent "least cost travel corridors." In an initial assessment of LiDAR topographic data the tools of GIS identified the "least cost corridor" that Collins would have followed between Mud Spring and the headwaters of Rush Creek. If the column stayed with the gentlest terrain available it would have followed established trails. They would have followed the Jules Cut-off up to its meeting with the overland trail at the North Platte and then traveled back to the east to Rush Creek which they could have followed up to the camp site. This hypothetical corridor would have been the easiest – but it was clearly not the route Collins followed!

As noted, on 7 February Collins had dispatched scouts to find where the Native community was camped so the routes that warriors had traveled to Mud Springs were probably known. Most of this travel had been hidden behind the hill to the east of the Station, but after several days of many commutes, Army

Fig. 7.2 The type of cannon used by Collins command was the 12-pdr Mountain Howitzer. The gun was relatively light-weight and could be towed behind a mule or horse or disassembled and components packed on mules or horses (authors' image)

scouts probably saw clear evidence of their adversaries' travel. With their gear and wagons, the Cavalry column may not have been able to follow the Indian paths, but clearly they had to cross the less than flat landscape.

East of the hill to the east of Mud Springs the terrain is rolling, with some hills, low bluffs and a couple of ephemeral spring-fed creeks. Since it offers limited vistas, Collins said the country he crossed was so broken that he feared for surprise Indian attacks. The hills on the south side of the Platte River are gently sloping, generally less than 25°. By contrast, exposed bedrock that surrounds the Rush Creek camp site, is steeper (25–35°) and exposed bedrock would have complicated access for such a large group traveling with wagons from all but a northerly direction. Thus, to explore the route the cavalry may have taken, we conducted a GIS corridor analysis to identify the most efficient route based on the distance and terrain between the station and the campsite.

Our modeled corridor is presented in Figure 7.1. A visual inspection of a shaded-relief image, derived from the DEM, along the travel corridor routes showed no evidence of ephemeral trail remnants still extant on the ground. Still, the reconstructed corridor presents some potentially useful insights. First, the hypothetical corridor is quite broad, indeed, more than a mile (1.6 km) wide in several spots. Looking for lost artifacts and gear that might provide "hard" archaeological evidence of the movement would involve searching a large area.

Fig. 7.3 (right) GIS derived viewsheds from the possible location of the Cheyenne camp north of the North Platte River, overlaid on the digital elevation model, emphasizes that Collins's command and the Cheyenne rearguard would not have seen one another until cresting a rise that became the Rush Creek battlefield (authors' original reconstruction)

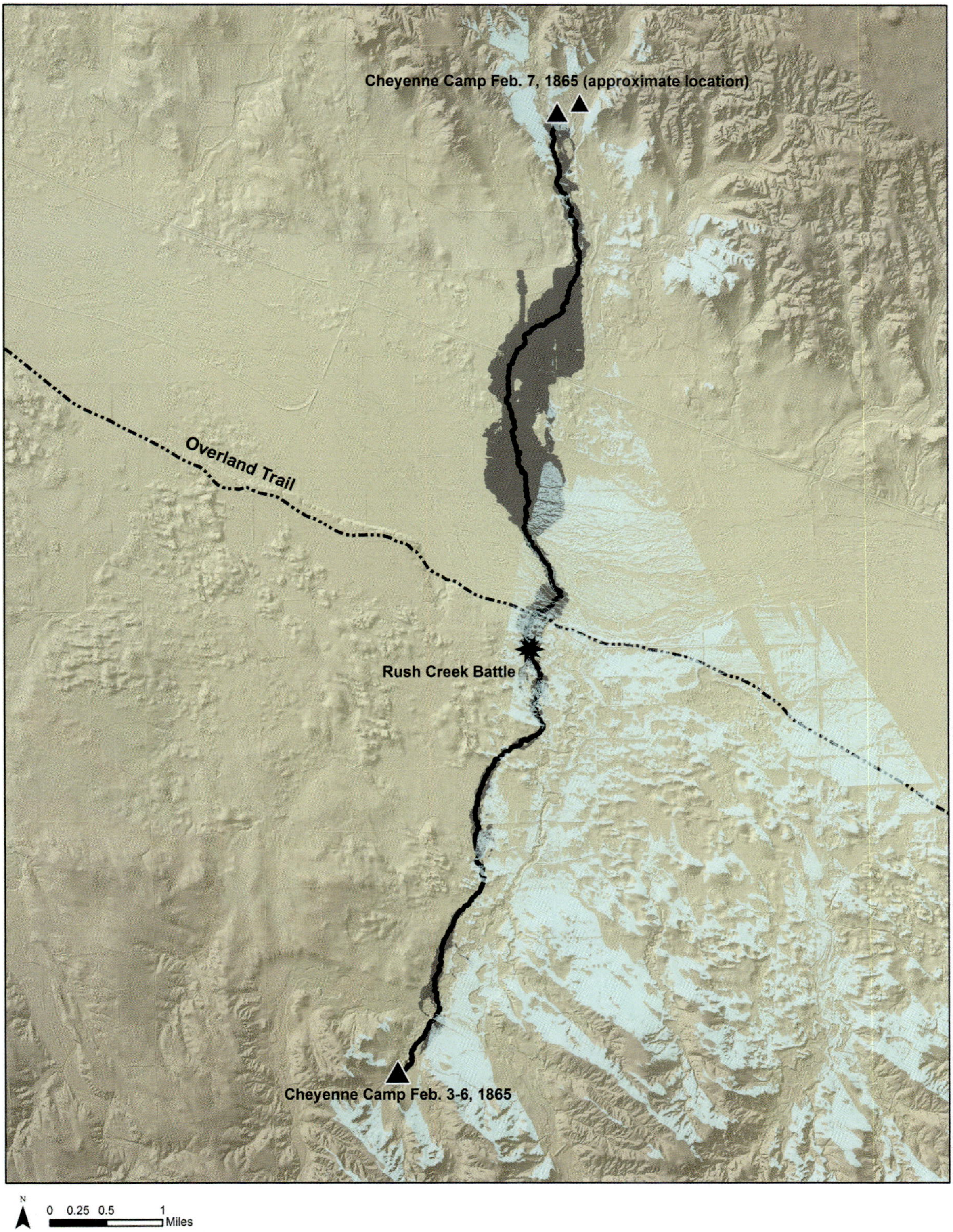
Cheyenne Camp Feb. 7, 1865 (approximate location)
Overland Trail
Rush Creek Battle
Cheyenne Camp Feb. 3-6, 1865
N
0 0.25 0.5 1
Miles

The size of the corridor strongly suggests that Collins and his men had ample flexibility. They could have moved around and away from challenging features. Topography would have had little influence on most of the route. The exception probably came toward the end of the trip. Steep, rocky ground north of the Rush Creek spring (called Deep Hole on modern geological maps) had two likely affects. First, as Collins drew close to the camp site, his view to the north toward the North Platte River was blocked. Had any Indians still been traveling away from their camp, Collins would not have seen them. Second, to avoid the rough country, Collins would have had to swing slightly north and enter the camp site from the south.

Discovery of the Rush Creek camp

Collins and his column found the site of the Cheyenne camp by the early afternoon of 8 February. By that time the camp was abandoned and the Cheyenne community had moved on. In his after-action report (Collins Report, OR) Collins gives a fairly full account of what he has his column found when they arrived at the Cheyenne camp site:

> "The camp was found where we expected at Rush Creek Springs. It was deserted, but there were evidences that it had been recently and hastily left; that they had been there about three days and were in great numbers. The camp covered several miles. Over 100 beef-cattle had been slaughtered in it. Empty oyster, meat, and fruit cans were plenty. Flour sacks, a quantity of codfish, and indications of the spoils of ranches and trains were scattered everywhere. Quantities of meat cut up for use and skins pegged down for drying and tanning were left upon the ground. Pressing forward on the now fresh trails, in four or five miles we reached the valley of the Platte, near the mouth of Rush Creek. When within a mile of the river we came in sight of the Indians on the other side scattered over the plains between the bluffs and the river, grazing their horses. There were no tepees or lodges, no travois or lodge poles, no women, children, or dogs in sight. They had all gone forward into the bluffs which at this point are about five miles north of the river, leaving the warriors only behind. The lodge trails were very broad and fresh, apparently made that morning and the evening before."

Using the corridor analysis again, we investigated the likely route taken by Collins and his men leaving Rush Creek Springs in pursuit of the Cheyenne (Fig. 7.3). The least-cost travel corridor, identified by the GIS, predictably leads north along the west bank of Rush Creek until reaching the bluffs where we assume the Cheyenne guards were waiting. Further analysis of the Cheyenne's view of the North Platte Valley revealed further insights into the Rush Creek battle. A GIS visibility or "viewshed" analysis, which creates a map of all visible locations from a single position on the landscape, was conducted using the high-resolution LiDAR DEM (Fig. 7.3). From this analysis, it became apparent that Collins and his men would not have been fully visible to the southward moving Cheyenne (and vice versa) until they reached the location where the battle occurred. An overlay analysis of the viewshed map with the least-cost travel corridor revealed that the two intersect at the location where artifacts from the battle were discovered.

When Cheyenne rear guards spotted the Army force moving in their direction in the afternoon of 8 February, warriors quickly moved to stop them. Leaving their home community at least somewhat exposed in a temporary camp, warriors recrossed the North Platte to engage the cavalry on the south side of the river. The appearance of these attackers, may have surprised Collins's force, but they quickly established a defensive position. Horses and wagons were assembled in a corral. Dismounted cavalrymen formed a perimeter. They deployed their cannon, threw up breastworks of some sort, and the battle of Rush Creek was begun.

8

The forces collide at Rush Creek

The fight that occurred when Indian and cavalry forces met near the mouth of Rush Creek involved the same parties who had been engaged at Mud Springs but the two battles were quite different. Mud Springs was attacked, defended, reinforced and secured in a series of rather simple operations. Rush Creek, by contrast, was a sharp engagement that involved creation of a defensive perimeter with hastily erected breastworks, followed by forceful attacks from selected terrain. There was, as well, a brief but focused use of artillery, and even an aggressive cavalry charge into enemy fire. All of this took place in the brief window that started late on the afternoon of 8 February 1865 and ending on the morning of 9 February when the sides parted and went in different directions.

The Rush Creek battle site and the battlespace area was largely produced by the accidental meeting of two forces. The Cheyenne were on the move. They had traveled north or downstream along Rush Creek to cross the frozen North Platte River in order to find new secure camping areas north of the river. Collins's command was following the trail of the Cheyenne from the Rush Creek camp site in hopes of finding them and inflicting additional punishment on the community – and perhaps recover some of the captured goods and animals. In Chapter 7 we discussed the movements of both the Cheyenne and Collins's cavalry column from Mud Springs.

In addition to being tactically different, the two battles of the North Platte Campaign also present rather different historical records. As noted, Mud Springs is a well-known location and the fighting that happened there is clearly recorded, although not with particularly rich detail. By contrast, the specific location of the Rush Creek action had been lost to history until historical and archaeological research in 2008 revealed its location and residues. The historical record of the Rush Creek fight is hardly detailed, but there is more to read about this fight than there is on Mud Springs. George Bent was still riding with his Cheyenne kinsmen when the sides met at Rush Creek and a letter he wrote to George Hyde on 4 May 1906 describes the conflict from the Indian perspective (Haack 2007, 33–4). Lt Col. Collins seems to have gathered his thoughts more fully after his hurried travel to Mud Springs since his after-action report on Rush Creek is fuller than his treatment of Mud Springs, where he had arrived tired and cold. A small group of cavalrymen also published information on their participation. Three of these were presented as veteran's account in the *National Tribune*, a monthly newspaper closely associated with the Grand Army of the Republic (GAR) and devoted to the interests of Civil War veterans (see Appendix 1 for full transcriptions of each account). Information relevant to the North Platte Campaign appeared in the mid-1890s so, like Bent's accounts, specific details may seem faded. The veterans who sent their reminiscences to the *National Tribune* (see Scott *et al.* 2011) wanted to record the facts of their service. This had been a central part of their Civil War experience and they might have wanted to make sure that their contributions were duly noted. Their recollections addressed a variety of personality and character issues and suggest that the soldiers who pursued the Cheyenne were sensitive to unit and state affiliation and to personal differences within their ranks. The goal of this chapter is to examine the historical accounts for information that exposes the tactical operations that made up the Rush Creek battle.

Beginning of the battle

Both the Indian forces and the soldiers who were pursuing them must have known that their adversaries were close and fully capable of serious combat, still historic records make it seem that Rush Creek fight was a surprise encounter.

George Bent did not record his recollections of Rush Creek until 50 years after the battle so, like cavalry veterans' recollections of the fight, his account may reflect faded memory and poorly controlled details. At the same time, having served with a Confederate artillery unit in Missouri and Arkansas, Bent was not a naïve observer (Haack 2007, 33–4).

> "Next morning about 2 o'clock in the evening Sioux Indian stood on high bluff and signaled with his buffalo robe soldiers were in sight. Everybody run for war horses. Everybody was always anxious to get to his enemy first to run off the stock or to capture something. When I got up on the bluff I saw train and soldiers in front and behind it coming up on the main road. The road runs south of the river. Indians were charging across the river like so many ants from where I was standing. I had fine field glasses that my father had given me in 1863, so I could see plain there were 4 companies with the train. They corralled the train soon as they seen Indians crossing over. They corralled near the river and in level place so the Indians could not get to them handy. I rode over with party and got south of the train behind sand hill about 1000 yards from them. The Indians were all around them. About 10 Indians rode under cover of the river bank and got within 200 yards of the soldiers before the soldiers seen them."

Lt Col. Collins's account of how the battle opened, in his after-action report in the Official Records of the War of the Rebellion (Hewett 1997, 203–33, Collins

Artillery and small arms in the North Platte Campaign

Artillery: The Mountain Howitzer

The 12-pdr Mountain Howitzer had been officially used by the United States Army since the 1830s (Mcfeaters 2008), and was much more popular on the Plains than it ever was in the main theaters of the Civil War. This was due to its relatively light weight compared to other pieces firing identical shot, and its ability to be either conventionally towed or broken down for transportation on horseback. The last feature was especially valuable for moving across country in the Plains.

The Mountain Howitzer could fire three different types of ammunition, all of which are relevant for discussion of the artillery fragments recovered at the Rush Creek battlefield. Shells were hollow cast iron balls 4.52 in (114.8 mm) in diameter containing a black powder bursting charge, and were designed to explode above the ground following a specific interval after firing. The shell would shatter into fragments of shrapnel, raining down upon the target (Greene and Scott 2004; Mcfeaters 2008). Similarly, case shot were hollow cast iron balls of the same size, but each contained 78 lead musket balls suspended in a hardened matrix of sulfur or resin. Case shot also contained a black powder bursting charge and exploded in a similar manner as shell, the musket balls providing additional shrapnel (Greene and Scott 2004; Mcfeaters 2008). "Gray" cast iron was chosen for use in these artillery projectiles, due to its low resistance to impact and consequent brittle mode of failure (Caporaso *et al.* 2007). Both shell and case shot used a hardened lead fuse called the Borman fuse. It had a series of gradations cast in one face, 1–5 to indicate the number of seconds of flight before the charge was to burst. The desired length of flight was determined by a table of fire fixed to the limber chest from which the ammunition was stored. The cut in the fuse exposed a powder train that burned in a spiral groove inside the fuse that regulated its flight time. The fuse was ignited by the round's propulsion charge when it was lit by a friction primer.

The third type of ammunition used in the Mountain Howitzer was canister. This projectile comprised a large tin can, 6.85 in (173.3 mm) in height and 4.52 in (114.8 mm) in diameter, which was supposed to contain 148 lead musket balls in four tiers (United States War Department 1851). The can would shatter upon firing, and the musket balls would disperse in a rapidly-expanding cone beyond the muzzle of the piece, the round in effect transforming the Howitzer into a giant shotgun (Mcfeaters 2008). Canister had the shortest range of all Mountain Howitzer ammunition, being intended for relatively close-quarters combat and useful between point-blank range and 250 yds (*c.* 230 m) (Mcfeaters 2008). In comparison, case shot and shell had maximum ranges of 800 yds and 1005 yds (*c.* 730 m and 920 m), respectively (Greene and Scott 2004). The use of lead balls in a canister round was intended to prevent damage to the bore of the Mountain Howitzer's bronze barrel (McFeaters 2008). However, canister shot containing iron balls was made for other 12-pdr guns (McKee and Mason 1980; 1995 Melton and Pawl 1994), and there is evidence that iron-ball canister was used in the mountain howitzer at Alkal Station (McFeaters 2008) and Rush Creek.

Firearms identification

Systematically recovered ammunition materials were analyzed with standard firearms identification (Heard 1997; Harris 1980; Haag 2006; Hatcher *et al.* 1977; Hatcher 1943; Gunther and Gunther 1935) procedures to determine the kind of arm, and where possible, the specific weapon that fired them. This then allowed determination of the number of different types of guns in use at the battle. Further, by comparing the unique qualities of firearm individual characteristics, they allow the identification of individual weapons. This capability is very important because, coupled with the precise artifact locations, identical individual characteristics can be used to trace the movements of individual weapons across the field of battle. With this information, patterns of movement can be established and the battle sequence can be more precisely interpreted.

Firearms types at the battles of Mud Springs and Rush Creek

Army troopers at Mud Springs and Rush Creek were armed with Spencer rifles or carbines, Wesson carbines, Springfield rifled muskets, Colt Navy revolvers, and other carbines like the Greene and Merrill, according to historic documents. The Springfield rifled muskets were likely the standard .58-caliber Minié ball musket. The 11th OVC records note that some Springfield rifled muskets were temporarily issued to Company I (S.O. No. 121, dated Hd Qtrs Western Sub. Dist. Neb. Ft Laramie, I.T., 20 February 1865), some muskets were the Enfield pattern (1st Lt Henry Averil Papers, Fort Riley, Kansas archives, hereinafter cited as Averil Papers). At least one Enfield musket is listed issued to and returned by Capt George Apt in the February 1865 (ordnance records kept by Lt Averil). The carbines identified as Greene and Merrill may have been the Joslyn .56-56-caliber carbine but none is well documented in the historic record. The ordnance records for the 11th OVC (Averil Papers) clearly state that most companies were issued Spencer Rifles or Wesson rifles. Pistols were the .44-caliber Army revolver which could have been either Colt or Remington brands. A few .36-caliber Navy revolvers were also issued for field use. Spencer rifles, although awkward for cavalry are known to have been issued to Companies E, F, G, and H of the 11th OVC per Averil's surviving ordnance records. Averil's records contain one clear indication of the armament used at Mud Springs and Rush Creek. Among the ordnance papers is 'Abstract of Materials and Etc. expended or consumed by the Eleventh OVC during the first quarter 1865.' The form denotes rounds expended in action at Mud Springs and Rush Creek. For Mud Springs 5422 rounds of elongated .52-caliber ball (Spencer cartridges) and 2324 rounds of elongated .44-caliber ball (Wesson cartridges) were expended or lost. The Rush Creek fight consumed 6100 Spencer rounds and 4000 Wesson rounds for a total of 11,522 Spencers and 6324 Wesson rounds fired or lost.

One interesting aspect of the firearms used by Collins's men is that the Wesson carbines had been privately purchased. Over 200 men of the 11th OVC voted to buy more reliable breech-loading weapons to replace the muzzle-loading rifled muskets they had first been issued as they were sent west in 1863 (Collins Papers, DPL). Collins acquired the guns and accoutrements including separate extractors from the B. Kittredge Company in May 1863. The government agreed to furnish cartridges for the .44-caliber rimfire guns if the men purchased their own weapons.

Indians were described as using repeating rifles, revolvers, and bows and arrows. Historic documents are less than precise in recording the warriors' armament. The archaeological record, dicussed here, provides the material evidence of the warriors' armament as well as confirming that of the Army forces.

Report, OR) was, of course, written without anything like the information or perspectives that Bent offered. Still, Collins's account parallels much of what Bent described. It also seems to indicate that Collins approached Rush Creek with no specific tactical plan. He also seems to have had no more than the general strategic plan he carried away from Ft Laramie. His goal was simply to open the flow of traffic along the Overland Trail:

> "Pressing forward on the now fresh trails, in four or five miles we reached the valley of the Platte, near the mouth of Rush Creek. When within a mile of the river we came in sight of the Indians on the other side scattered over the plains between the bluffs and the river, grazing their horses. There were no tepees or lodges, no travois or lodge poles, no women, children, or dogs in sight. They had all gone forward into the bluffs which at this point are about five miles north of the river, leaving the warriors only behind.

> The lodge trails were very broad and fresh, apparently made that morning and the evening before.
>
> It was now clear we had underestimated the numbers against us. With a field-glass they could be distinctly seen and examined. There were at least 2,000 warriors in sight. It was evident that all the hostile Indians that had been committing depredations and holding the country along the South Platte were concentrated here. The river was about half a mile wide and frozen over. While we were looking for a crossing they save us the trouble by commencing to swarm down to the river-banks and come over on the ice, not opposite, but one or two miles above and below us. We had barely time to corral our train before they were upon us on every side. The position chosen was the best we could get, but there were many little sand ridges and hollows under cover of which they could approach us. A very great change had come over the men since the morning of the fight at Mud Springs. They were rested and free from excitement, had confidence in their officers, obeyed orders, and went to work with a will."

An enlisted trooper's recollection and assessment of how the Rush Creek battle opened was presented by George Rowan, formerly of Company D, 7th IVC and reported in the 30 January 1890 issue of the *National Tribune* (see Appendix 1 for full transcription). Rowan had arrived at Mud Springs on 7 February and offered his comments to correct information that had been presented in another *National Tribune* article by E. M. Drake who had been a trooper in Co. B, 11th OVC. Rowan said:

> "Therefore, on the morning of the second day we followed their trail northeast to the North Platte where the waters of Rush Creek empty into that river, and the stream being frozen over, the Colonel's orders were to march on to meet the Indians, who by this time were coming out of the hills on the opposite side of the river in great numbers, which we estimated at 50 to our one, and who would have met us on the ice where the greatest victory the Indians ever won, and the greatest slaughter that ever occurred in the West would have taken place (the Custer massacre not excepted) had not nearly all the commissioned officers of the command earnestly advised the Colonel to fall back to a commanding position on the banks of Rush Creek, where the two days' siege took place, known as the Rush Creek fight, to which Mr. Drake refers."

Tactical operations of Rush Creek combat

For the Cavalry side, Lt Col. Collins began the Rush Creek fighting from a defensive stance (Fig. 8.1). In his after-action report (Collins report, OR), he says that after his column had been discovered,

Fig. 8.1 Cheyenne biopictograph of warriors attacking entrenched soldiers with a wagon corral (courtesy History Colorado, Cheyenne Sketcthbook, 10036164)

> "We camped on the battle-ground and continued to prepare and occupy favorable positions during the night and morning. About sunrise on the 9th they began to come over above and below, until some 400 mounted warriors were counted, without any apparent diminution of the number left on the north side of the river. They found us ready, skirmished about for awhile, exchanged a few shots, and then began to recross and put off rapidly for the bluffs. At noon very few were to be seen."

Collins also added:

> "Sharpshooters were pushed out, and the hillocks commanding the camp occupied, and rifle-pits dug upon them. The Indians of the plains are the best skirmishers in the world. In rapidity of movement, sudden wheeling and hanging over steep and difficult ground, no trained cavalry can equal them. Hunting the buffalo is the best possible school. We were not strong enough to charge or scatter. It was necessary to be prudent, and at first take the defensive. They dashed up very boldly, but soon fell back from our bullets, and resorted to their old game of skulking and sharpshooting. At this game they were well met by our men."

Virtually all of the recorded observations of the Rush Creek fighting mention exchange of gunfire along the perimeter that the cavalry had established around their corralled wagon (Haack 2007, 33–4; see Appendix 1 for various accounts of the fighting).

A. G. Shaw, former 11th OVC trooper who was interviewed by Eli Ricker in Valentine, Nebraska on 1 September 1 1907 (Jenson 2005), recalled what would have been the center of the cavalry position where they corralled the wagons and maneuvered them so that wagon boxes met and interlocked the wheels providing an protective front on all but the north or river side of the position.

All the Rush Creek veterans also mentioned an excavated breastwork or rifle pits around the cavalry perimeter. Shaw told Ricker (Jenson 2005) that soldiers were ordered to dig rifle pits in the frozen ground within the wagon enclosure so the men could shoot from under the wagons.

George Rowan's account (see Appendix 1) contradicts Shaw's by saying that digging the "works" was an easy matters as the soil was very sandy and easily removed. Clearly these contradictory statements reflect the need to evaluate all sources critically to determine whose are the more accurate.

From the Indian side, George Bent viewed the fighting from a distance of some 1000 yds (around 900 m). He was not alone at that distance, which would have been beyond the easy range of the trooper guns. He also makes it clear that some Cheyenne fighters drew closer to the enemy positions and fought from natural draws and other topographic irregularities. These descriptions are matched by recollections of cavalrymen. George Nelson, a veteran of Co. I 11th OVC gave this account of the Rush Creek combat:

> "True, we had a very strong position, but they outnumbered us at least 10 to one; were well armed, well mounted, cunning and brave; in fact, they fought like old warriors from away back. About 200 to 300 yards from our ditch was what seemed to be a long, low place, or dry branch, where the grass and sagebrush had grown very rank, and the dead grass having fallen down, afforded good concealment for the redskins."

Artillery at Rush Creek

Before leaving Ft Laramie, Lt Col. Collins decided to include a single 12-pdr Mountain Howitzer in the rescue force (see Fig. 7.2). Collins clearly thought that the cannon could still prove useful since he ordered it into the column that moved toward Rush Creek.

Several observers recalled the use of the cannon at Rush Creek, but the role that artillery played in the fighting seems uncertain. Collins himself barely mentioned artillery in his after-action report. George Bent (Haack 2007, 33–4), who had served as an Confederate artillerist early in the Civil War and before he returned to his mother's band, also barely mentions use of the cannon in his recollections, noting that the cannon was used with grape shot (*sic*) but only wounded one warrior, Yellow Nose, a Lakota, who was struck in the leg.

Army veterans of the battle, however, felt that the use of the Howitzer had been important. By George Rowan's account:

> "Much of the credit is due to the Lieutenant of the 11th Ohio Cav. For the able manner in which he handled the little gun, which no doubt saved the lives of us all. ... In fact, the only charge made was by the soldiers, who

> charged to dislodge Indians, who had crept so close to our breastworks that they were pouring volleys of lead and arrows into our lines ..."

In sum, then, it is certain that artillery was employed at Rush Creek, but the location of the cannon and the role it may have played in resolution of the fight seem quite uncertain.

Cavalry action at Rush Creek

The Army column was composed of mounted soldiers so the entire Rush Creek battle was a cavalry operation but, as discussed earlier, the troopers used their horses for mobility and usual fought on foot. Even in eastern battles of the Civil War mounted cavalry charges were very rare (Griffith 1986, 42). The fact that Rush Creek involved an organized cavalry charge into Indian positons is one of the battle's most unusual tactical features (Fig. 8.2).

In his after-action report, Collins (Collin Report, OR) presents the cavalry charge as a major factor in the battle:

> "At one point we were greatly annoyed by a party of ten or fifteen behind a little knoll about 400 yards distant, and it became evident they must be dislodged. A detail was made of sixteen mounted men, part from the detachment of Company D, Seventy Iowa Cavalry, and part from a detachment of the First Battalion, Eleventh Ohio Volunteer Cavalry. The party was placed in command of Lieutenant Patton, Eleventh Ohio Volunteer Cavalry, and he was ordered to charge at full speed, revolvers in hand, to clear out the Indians behind the hillock, and, having done, so wheel and return immediately. It was admirably done; the skulkers were routed and fled. In the meantime there were from 150 to 200 Indians on the rising ground beyond the contested hillock, which was about midway between us

Fig. 8.2 A mounted soldier of the 11th Ohio Volunteer Cavalry showing his Spencer rifle, cavalry saber, and revolver, *c.* 1865 (courtesy Wyoming State Archives, Bretney Collection, 25810)

> and them. When they saw the charge they swarmed down to save their men, and our party had a short hand-to-hand fight with their advance and then wheeled and returned as ordered. In this charge we lost two men, Private John A. Harris, Company D, Seventh Iowa Cavalry who fell in the fight, and Private William H. Hartshorn, Company C, Eleventh Ohio Volunteer Cavalry a veteran, who was on a very spirited horse, and either his own ardor or inability to control his horse or both, led him forward into the thickest of the Indians, and we saw him no more alive. Many Indians were killed and wounded in this charge. They fell immediately back before our fire as the charging party returned. A small party immediately went out and brought in the body of Harris. The Indians had not time to scalp him or take his arms or clothing, and they were brought in with him. The body of Hartshorn was found next morning about one mile from our camp, horribly mutilated, with ninety-seven arrows sticking in it. It is not unlikely that some chief of note was killed by him, or someone else in the charge, and that each one of his relations and friends put an arrow in him and left it, as it is sometimes their custom. Both bodies were brought to Fort Laramie for burial. I desire especially to call attention to the conduct of Lieutenant Patton and his little body of men. The charge was a very gallant one, and the desired objects were fully accomplished. Toward night we could not bring the Indians, in reach of our fire. They retired behind the hills and were returning across the Platte until dark, when very few seemed to be on the south side of the river."

George Nelson also recalled the cavalry charge in his *National Tribune* piece stating that from 200 to 300 yards (*c.* 180–275 m) from the army position there was a low spot which offered cover and concealment to the warriors. From this position they fired on the soldiers. Nelson's account parallels the official account well, but his description of the charge, loss of the two men, and the retrograde movement, under fire, of the troopers offers more detail.

The battle took place on the 8 February and Collins reported that only minor skirmishing occurred during the morning of 9 February, until about noon. At 2 pm that day the command left its position and moved about 15 miles (25 km) up the Platte River toward Fort Mitchell. On the morning of 10 February the command was split – Lt Brown, taking the Rush Creek wounded and the Fort Mitchell home command, marched to Fort Mitchell and then on to Fort Laramie. Collins took the remaining troops back to Mud Springs Station to pick up the sick and wounded there and transport them to Fort Laramie. Collins, with about 75 men, marched on 10 February to Pole Creek [*sic* Lodgepole Creek] to determine the station's condition and ascertain the status of the telegraph line repair party of the 7th IVC. Collins completed his return journey to Fort Laramie on 14 February (Collins Report, OR) thus ending their role in the battles of the North Platte River valley. The Cheyenne, too, had ended their role for the time being, moving north of the river in to the safer sand hill area of northwestern Nebraska and eastern Wyoming.

9

Firing line landscapes: archaeology of the Rush Creek battle

Based on historical accounts, an interesting set of combat issues can be investigated archaeologically at the Rush Creek battlefield. The battle seems to have been a hastily organized confrontation that neither side had planned. Once the fighting started, the adversaries used terrain for defense and attack along a protective perimeter. Additionally, there was an overnight bivouac with some quickly prepared breastworks around a circle of wagons and corralled horses. Finally, the battle featured some rounds of cannon fire and a bold, but brief, cavalry attack. Assessing those actions archaeologically depended on locating the battlefield and that turned out to be a challenge.

The location of the fighting at Mud Springs was never in doubt. Along with the station's role as a major watering stop, Pony Express station, and telegraph link, the Mud Springs battlefield was known and celebrated. The Rush Creek fight, by contrast, did not share that kind of recognition. It was "near" some generally known features of the overland trail, but it actually took place in an unmarked and unremarkable location. When the fighting ended both sides left the field and its specific location was forgotten.

While investigating the Mud Springs fight we started looking for the area where the Rush Creek encounter had taken place. Guided by historical accounts we visited locations that fitted the description of the battle terrain but found neither traces of combat nor explicit terrain we could link to the historic descriptions. Our major clue was a reference to the "white bluffs" on the north side of the river where the Cheyenne and their allies camped on 7 February 1865. Analysis of aerial imagery, topographic maps, and historical sources only provided a general area in which to search. This area of Nebraska, south of the North Platte River, contains numerous similarly disposed drainage patterns and rolling prairie that, on first glance, are largely undistinguished. In 2008 we decided to involve students in the University of Nebraska-Lincoln (UNL) Summer Field School in one more day of searching and systematic metal detection of our best choice locations. This time we were guided by local rancher Pete Peters and Morrill County historian Bill Vogler. With their sensitive familiarity of local terrain they led us to an area on Cedar Creek

Metal detecting survey

A primary research goal of the Mud Springs and Rush Creek Battlefield investigations was to locate and define the limits of the battlefields. As such it was necessary to determine where artifacts are found, but also where they are not found. The first requirement, then, was to develop field procedures that were capable of examining the entire extent of the battlefield. It was assumed that most surviving artifacts of war would be either metallic or associated with metal, and metal detectors were employed as an inventory tool based on the success of the technique at Little Bighorn Battlefield National Monument (Scott and Fox 1987; Scott *et al.* 1989) and employed widely since then. The use of metal detectors operated by knowledgeable people has overwhelmingly proven its value (Connor and Scott 1998; Espenshade *et al.* 2002; Foard and Curry 2014) and is now a common tool employed in archaeological investigations of battlefields, campsites, and many other historic sites on both sides of the Atlantic.

There are many survey techniques and methods that can be employed when using metal detectors. The first requirement is that the detectors be of good quality and capable of discriminating different metal types. Generally metal detecting includes three sequential operations: survey, recovery and recording. During survey detector operators are lined up and systematically sweep a transect or corridor with the detector to locate all metal artifacts in their assigned area. Artifact targets or finds are marked, usually with fiberglass or other non-metallic shaft pin flags. A recovery crew excavates artifact locations marked by pin flags and leaves the artifacts in place for recording. The recovery team usually consists of excavators and metaldetector operators. Detector operators provide pinpointing and depth information to the excavator, thereby allowing a careful and accurate approach to the artifact. The metal artifact finds holes can also be used as proxies for random shovel testpittting. As such they provide information on soil formation and stratification to the depth of the metal artifact find. Once the artifact is exposed then a recording team documents the find using standard archaeological recording techniques, such as recording the find location with a total station transit or a global positioning system, noting depth, soil conditions, field artifact identification, and recording other appropriate field and provenience data.

Fig. 9.1 University of Nebraska archaeological field school students metal detecting the site of the Rush Creek battlefield (authors' image)

Fig. 9.2 Spencer and Wesson cartridges and cartridge cases were found in significant numbers and clusters at Rush Creek indicating the fighting positions of the soldiers (authors' image)

which they pointed out had formerly been called Rush Creek. They also convinced us that it might match the historic description of the Rush Creek battlefield. Working with Field School students for most of a day of unsuccessful systematic metal detection, we were about to give up when we discovered a group of .56–56 and .44 caliber cartridge cases – from exactly the gun types used in the Rush Creek fighting.

To amplify the initial discovery and clarify the distribution of battle debris we returned to the area in 2009 and involved another crew of Field School students in a systematic metal detection survey (Fig. 9.1). An area of some 30,000 m^2 was searched at 5 m interval. Individual finds were recorded with a GPS unit. Civil War era finds were collected for analysis. This methodology was suited to investigation of the battle for at least two reasons. First, by affording systematic inspection of the entire battle zone, the survey showed that no clear or definitive traces of "breastworks" or other defensive constructions had survived in the sandy soil. Second, and much more positively, metal detection revealed clusters of cartridges, cases and bullets that marked combat areas. This information revealed where the opposing forces – and especially the cavalrymen – were located, where they aimed, and the terrain they used for cover. Presenting those data is the special focus of this chapter.

The land immediately next to the North Platte River was the focus of emigrant travel along the overland trail because is quite flat and easily traversed. Within a half a mile (0.8 km) or less from the river, however, the land begins to slope upward in a rolling climb toward the rocky outcrops that form the margins of the North Platte valley (Scott *et al.* 2011). The fighting at Rush Creek occurred near the meeting of the flat river course and the sloping valley sides. This part of the valley has many large, relatively flat expanses, but there are also low, round-topped hills along the margins of Cedar Creek. Large hills rise less than a mile (1.6 km) west of the battlefield. In several areas, the flat land of the braided river course is separated from the valley slope by banks up to 10 ft (3 m) high. The implication of this constellation of features means that the battlefield seems open, but, in detail, it actually presents terrain that offered cover and protection to engaged forces.

Cheyenne sentinels spotted the oncoming troops of Collins's command on the afternoon of 8 February. They sent word to the mobile camp to move the women and children and others to shelter in the white limestone bluffs. The warriors assembled, perhaps as many as 2000 according to Army accounts, but this is likely a gross exaggeration. The warriors began to move south across the river to meet the threat posed by the advancing column. The warriors quickly surrounded the soldiers who had, likewise, spotted the

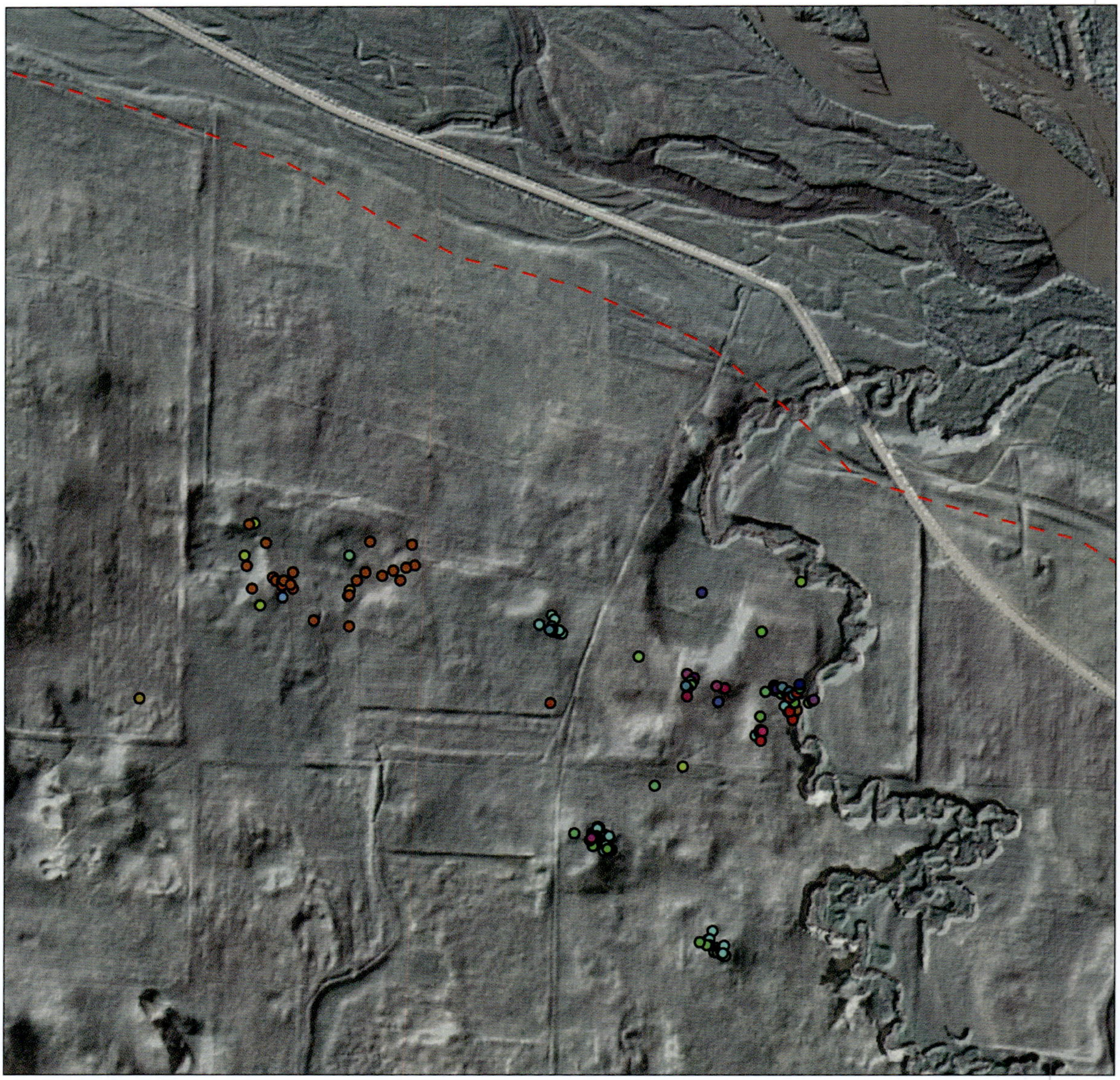

Fig. 9.3 The distribution of artifacts from Rush Creek is overlain on a high resolution LiDAR image. The colors other than orange and yellow denote the find locations of the soldier-fired cartridge cases. Note how they tend to cluster in association with small sand dunes. These dunes are likely remnants of rifle pits or entrenchments dug by the soldiers during the battle (see text). The orange dots represent the distribution of artillery shell and case shot shrapnel fragments. The single yellow dot is an iron canister shot ball. The red dashed line indicates the path of the overland trail along the river (authors' original reconstruction)

Indians as the last of the families and captured horses and cattle were crossing the frozen river.

Viewshed analysis (see Fig. 7.3) suggests the warrior sentinels and the advancing soldier column observed one another about the same time. That occurred essentially on what became the battlefield. Collins and his men knew they were traversing ground that would lead them to the North Platte and the well-worn overland trail. The command, having spent almost 3 years protecting this very trail, were well aware of where they were, but the meeting of the two opposing groups near the mouth of Rush Creek was a surprise to both as

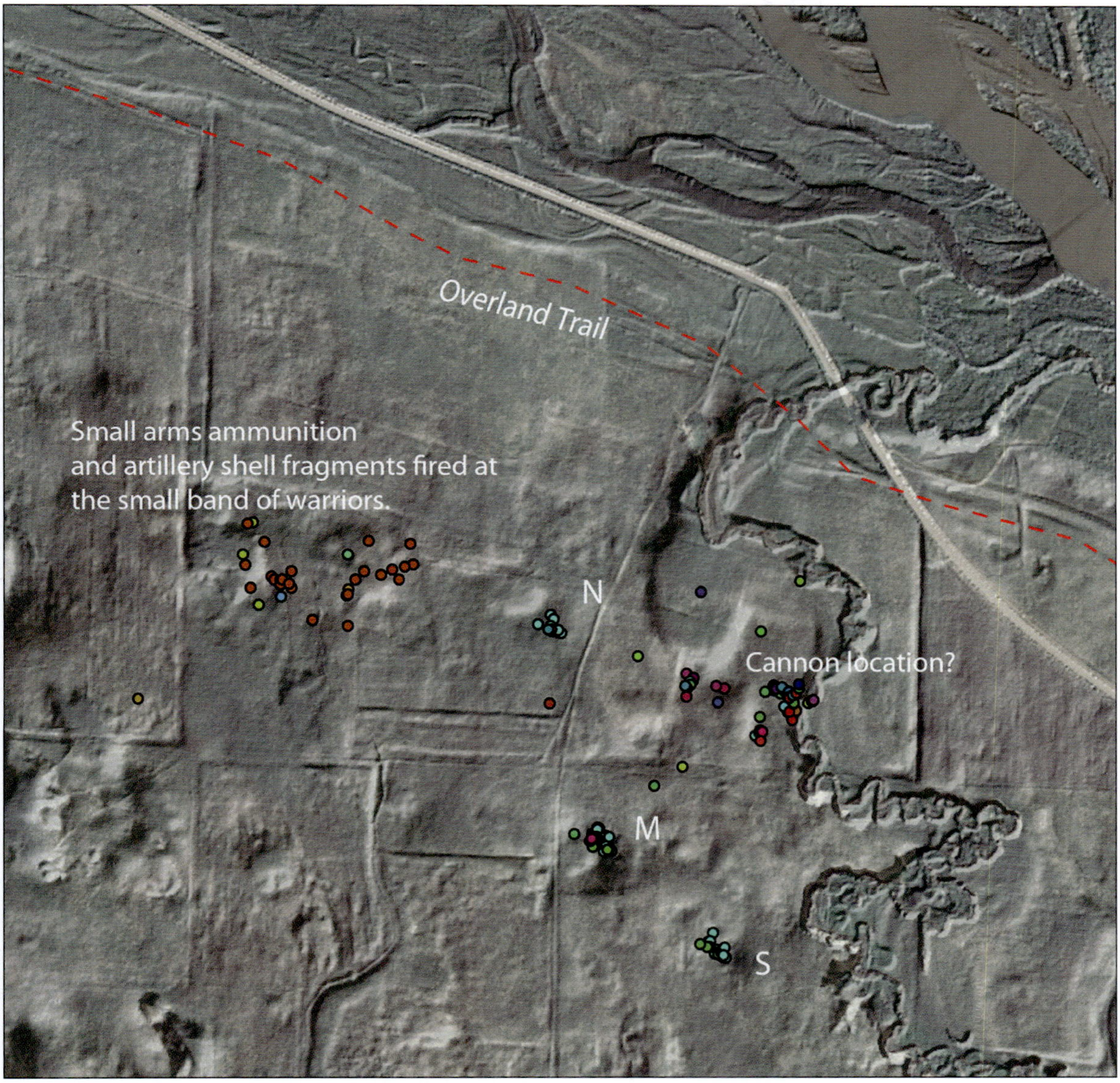

Fig. 9.4 The Rush Creek battle archaeological evidence shows the Cheyenne warriors held the higher ground, likely just out of the soldiers' gunshot range. There they held the entrenched soldiers at bay while their families moved the camp further north and to safety. One group of warriors attempted to flank the soldiers by using the banks of an old river terrace as cover. They were discovered and after a mounted charge by the soldiers was unable to dislodge them, the Mountain Howitzer was brought to bear on the warrior group. The artillery effectively ended the battle with the warriors moving north to rejoin their families (see text for annotations) (authors' original reconstruction)

neither had planned for an attack or defense. Both groups acted as they had been trained and deployed their forces according to their cultural construct of warfare.

As the warriors recrossed the river they began to fan out, likely in smaller self-assembled fighting units. They minimized their risk of suffering casualties by taking the high ground around the column advancing along the banks of Rush Creek. That high ground is the rising hills that flank the Rush Creek valley. The hills rise 30 ft (9 m) or more above the relatively flat valley floor and are at distances from the creek of a few hundred to more than 2000 ft (up to 600 m). The warriors largely occupied these hilltops. While their rifle and carbine fire was largely ineffective at inflicting causalities among the soldiers it did cause the command to halt their advance and form a defensive posture.

Even if the number of warriors is exaggerated by a factor of 5–10, the soldiers' perception of being severely outnumbered, as recounted in the historic accounts, led Collins to halt the command, bunch or circle the wagons, and have the men of the command find or create a defensible perimeter from which they could return fire at the warriors positions on the surrounding hills.

As evidenced in the historic accounts, shooting was at long range with little or no effect on either party. The only consequence was the soldiers were pinned down by the Cheyenne until a valorous display was promulgated by a small party of warriors. This party, of perhaps ten young warriors, crept to within a few hundred yards of the soldiers' defensive position undercover of the old terrace edge, referred to as a "bluff" in the historic record.

With the warriors in close firing range Collins ordered elements of his command, consisting of 16 soldiers, to mount and charge in order to drive the warriors away. It was done in the best tradition of cavalry tactics, but failed miserably, as did most mounted charges against Indians. Two runaway cavalry mounts cost their riders their lives and only support from the Mountain Howitzer saved the cavalrymen from apparent imminent destruction. One warrior might have been wounded in the melée. The warriors made their escape and, for all practical purposes, the battle was over. Both sides seemed to think they achieved, if not a victory, at least accomplishment of its goal. The Cheyenne camp was safely across the river and in protected terrain. The soldiers perceived they had driven the Cheyenne away from the trail and protected its occupants and travelers as well as reopened the all-important telegraph line.

Archaeological expression of the battlefield

The metal detecting archaeological investigations recovered nearly 100 cartridges cases (largely Army-related), lead bullets, burst artillery shell fragments and a canister shot ball, all in a patterned distribution (Scott *et al.* 2011). The battle-related cartridge cases, Spencers and Wessons, were found in three spatially discrete clusters within the army defense area, clearly indicating these two firearm types predominated in the volunteers' armament during the Rush Creek Battle (Figs 9.2 and 9.3). The same firearm types were also found at Mud Springs (Bleed and Scott 2009), and Wesson and Spencer cartridge case firing pin marks matched between the two battlefields, confirming that the Army employed these firearms at both battlefields. The firing pin matches clearly link the two battles and the specific guns used by the combatants. The clusters are identified for convenience as the southern group, middle group, and northern group. In addition two fired and two unfired Spencer rounds, as well as four fired Wesson rounds, were scattered along a line west of the creek and east of the northern group.

Small arms evidence

The northern cartridge case group is represented by six Wesson cartridge cases representing five individual guns (Guns = 16, 17, 18, 19 and 20). A .58-caliber Minié ball, unfired and dropped, was found among the Wesson rounds (N on Fig 9.3). The cartridge cases and lead bullet were found on the east side of the military crest of a low dune-like feature that has an axis trending from northwest to southeast. A "military crest" is just behind the top of a hill, dune, or other feature. It is the area where a combatant can find cover from incoming fire, but still be in a position to fire his weapon at attackers. The artifacts were spread out over an area of approximately 44 × 34 m suggesting the shooters were widely spaced in this area.

The middle cartridge case cluster (M on Fig. 9.3) was located on the eastern military crest of a long, high dune-like mound and was also the farthest west of the cartridge case clusters. The dune trended in a mostly northwest to southeast line. Twenty-two guns were represented by the nine Spencer cases, 24 Wesson fired cases, and an unfired musket percussion cap. The nine Spencer cartridge cases represent five individual Spencers and were recovered in two separate groups within the cluster, one to its the north-west side. The areas within this cluster are separated by some 13 m and it is clear that guns 1, 8 and 9 moved between the two. Sixteen Wessons are represented by 24 fired .44-caliber cartridge cases. The cartridge cases were found scatted over an area of approximately 35 m north-west to south-east and 26.5 m east to west.

The southern cartridge case cluster, (S on Fig. 9.3) located on the military crest on the north side of a low sandy, east to west trending ridge, represents eight Spencers and seven Wessons. The 16 Spencer cartridge cases were also distributed in two groups within the southern cluster. One group, on the western side of the ridge, was found within a 7.5 × 7.5 m area and all eight individual Spencers we identified are represented in the group. The second Spencer group was found on the eastern side of the ridge in an area extending 8.3 m east to west and 6 m north to south. The two Spencers represented here moved between the two areas. Spencers 1 and 5 also moved between the southern group and the middle group based on the presence of matching firing pin imprints on Spencer cartridge cases found in both clusters.

Six Wessons are also represented in the southern cartridge case cluster. Gun 2 fired 18 rounds, Gun 3: 31 rounds, Gun 4: 2 rounds, Gun 5: 6 rounds, and Guns 8 and 13 fired 1 round each for a total 60 .44-caliber rounds fired in this position. The Wesson rounds were found clustered in an area of approximately 30.25 m east to west and 15.5 m north to south. Four Wessons represented in the southern cluster were also noted by matching firing pin imprints in the middle cluster.

Found west of the Creek, but west of the northern group and main artifact distribution, were four Wesson cartridge cases, and two unfired Spencer cartridges and two cartridge cases. The Wesson fired cartridge cases represent four individual firearms, two by only a single example. The other two had matches to Wesson rounds fired the middle and in southern clusters. The two fired Spencer cartridge cases were both fired in a gun that also fired rounds in the middle and southern clusters.

Collins had between 160 and 180 officers and men in his command and, of that number, 12 were officers. The officers would have been armed with revolvers and the enlisted men with shoulder fired arms, mostly carbines, as well as revolvers. If Collins followed standard procedure then, once he took his defensive position and corralled his wagons, approximately a quarter of the enlisted men would have been detailed to guard the wagons and hold or guard the horses. They would likely have done little firing, and the Mountain Howitzer gun crew, one officer and five men, likely did no firing with small arms, thus leaving about 108–123 men for deployment on the defense perimeter. The archaeological record indicates there were a minimum of 25 Wesson carbines, ten Spencer rifles, and at least one .58-caliber rifled musket for a minimum total of 36 guns. This represents 29–33% of the likely number of men deployed on the defense perimeter.

In comparing the Rush Creek firearms minimum number derived from the archaeological record to other sites it can be seen that there are striking similarities. The 1876 Little Bighorn battlefield archaeological project firearm artifact analysis identified 69 .45-caliber army carbines at Custer Field, out of approximately 210 that were in the hands of the annihilated soldiers, ie, a 32.85% recovery rate. The associated Reno-Benteen defense site analysis determined that a minimum of 62 .45-caliber carbines were present out of approximately 350 men likely armed with the M1873 Springfield carbine, for a 17.71% recovery rate. The average for the two Little Bighorn related units is 28.47% (Scott *et al.* 1989).

Archaeological investigations at the 1877 Big Hole battle, where comparable studies were conducted, recovered evidence for the use of a minimum of 90 .45-caliber rifles and carbines for a 41% recovery rate of the total likely present during the battle. This is the highest recovery and identification rate on any site where comparable firearm identification techniques have been employed (Scott 1994).

The range of archaeologically identified firearm minimums range from 17.71% to 41%, and the Rush Creek analysis of 29–33% falls neatly near the middle of the range. The Rush Creek sample is consistent with the other comparable sites, further confirming the validity of the archaeologically recovered firearms sample, with the emphasis on the fact that the metal detecting methods are designed to collect about a 20–30% sample of artifacts at any given site. An important point regarding Rush Creek is that it was not collected or metal detected prior to the current investigation, and most of the site had never been ploughed, making it a near pristine site.

Metal detecting recovered very few lead bullets associated with the Rush Creek Battle. The presence of a single unfired and dropped .58-caliber Minié ball indicates at least one military type rifled musket was present with Collins's command. Two bullets, one a .44-caliber fired in a Henry and the other, a *c.* .50-caliber rifle ball were found embedded in the army position suggesting the warriors possessed a Henry and a .50-caliber rifle, and these two guns at least were within range of the entrenched command. A single .36-caliber unfired and dropped pistol bullet, likely made at the St Louis Arsenal, may be a lost round associated with the soldiers' charge on the warriors that crept within a few hundred yards of the command or a round lost by a warrior who occupied some of the high ground that overlooked the soldiers' positions.

A single lead chunk, exhibiting cut marks and manual manipulation may be a lost item from one of the warriors who employed the cover of a bank to come close to the army defenses. The lead item is of a weight that it could be cast or even formed by rolling or pounding into a bullet of approximately .58- to .69-caliber. This piece of lead may have been part of a personal kit and meant to function as raw material to form ersatz ammunition, perhaps for a trade musket or a captured army musket.

Three other lead balls of .69-caliber were found on the west edge of the artillery case shot burst pattern. These are likely case shot balls that were scattered when the round exploded in the air over or near the warriors who gathered around the body of Private Hartshorn (see below). This conjecture assumes the recollections of soldiers are accurate. At least the artillery case shot fragments and the lead case shot balls' position indicate a case shot was fired and burst some 350 yards (*c.* 340 m)or more west of the army defense area.

Artillery evidence

The use of the Mountain Howitzer during the battle of Rush Creek is only occasionally referenced in the available sources. In Lt Col. Collins's after-action report, he mentions only that the Howitzer was "admirably served" by Lt Brown, but was less effective than desired due to problems with the ammunition: "many of the shells failing to burst at all and some bursting at the muzzle of the gun". He goes on to attribute this problem to the ammunition being in storage at Fort Laramie for too long, some of it having been "in the magazine for eight or ten years" (Collins Report, OR). However, as discussed above, in 1890, the *National Tribune* published two accounts of participants in the battle. In one of them, George Rowan (Company D, 7th IVC at the time of Rush Creek), declares that "the manipulation of the small gun" and the charge of Lt Patton and his group, "is what saved our lives." The *National Tribune* published another soldier account in 1898, that of David Peck of Company H, 11th OVC. Peck declares on two separate occasions that the Howitzer was double-shotted, once when describing the beginning of the battle when groups of Indians were swarming across the North Platte River (and describes how "a swath was cut through them") and a second time on the morning of 9 February, when he says that a double shot from the Howitzer drove away a group of Indians clustering around an object on a bluff "about a quarter of a mile away". This turned out to be the mutilated body of William Hartshorn. However, Peck also states that "a few solid shot were fired", which was a type of ammunition not meant to be fired by the Mountain Howitzer, and was not included in a conventional ammunition chest (Greene and Scott 2004). Thus, the primary sources alone leave no clear and unambiguous picture of the tactical use of the Mountain Howitzer at Rush Creek.

The reference to double-shotting the gun is likely the result of poor memory or a literary exaggeration, as it was not a standard practice to double shot a Mountain Howitzer with canister shot, and it was not feasible to do so with explosive case or shell. However, Collins's concerns over the faulty ammunition rounds failing to burst on discharge can, in part, be archaeologically evaluated with the recovered physical evidence. No artillery rounds or fragments of rounds were found to the north (Fig. 9.3) and, if fired in that direction, especially at warriors on the ice and crossing the river, it is unlikely that evidence could be found of those rounds. The only possible archaeological evidence for a round being fired to the north is the tin strap fragment recovered on the higher ground in the Army defense area, suggesting the gun was located nearby (see Fig 9.3). The strap would have broken and fallen to the ground soon after being fired and its location is consistent with it dropping to the ground if the gun was fired to the north. On the other hand, since the firing of the Mountain Howitzer at the warrior cluster is verified, with over 20 case shot fragments (Figs 9.3 and 9.4), the strap fragment location is not inconsistent with the cannon being fired in a westerly direction, if the strap blew off to the side upon exiting the muzzle. At a minimum, one 12-pdr case shot round was fired at the warriors, and there is no question it performed as stipulated, breaking into a large number of shrapnel fragments, and distributing the fragments in an area of 200 × 150 m. At least one round of non-regulation canister was also fired, it also performing as required. A canister round recovered over 600 m from the presumed gun location (near the tin strap), assuming the gun was not moved at some point (see Fig. 9.3). The canister round is likely a piece that fell to earth after reaching its maximum range and terminal velocity. If there were rounds that failed to explode they are not present in the archaeological record. Either Collins exaggerated his claim to faulty artillery ammunition or the investigation failed to find these rather large dense iron objects. Certainly there is no archaeological evidence for rounds bursting near the muzzle of the gun, as no shell or case shot fragments were recovered in any area related to the army defense perimeter.

The use of a canister round during the battle may imply that Cheyenne warriors approached to within 250 yds (*c.* 230 m) of the Howitzer's firing position, as this was the maximum effective range of this type of ammunition (Mcfeaters 2008; United States War Department 1851). However, the use of canister for psychological effect cannot be entirely ruled out, as suggested by the account of David Peck in his *National Tribune* piece, which describes the use of the Howitzer after the battle to disperse a few Cheyenne from around William Hartshorn's body. Though the accuracy of the Rush Creek soldier accounts published in the *National Tribune* should be carefully evaluated, due to their temporal separation from the events they describe, the use of artillery on the Plains for this purpose is attested to by Capt. Eugene Ware (1994) in his account of the Indian War of 1864.

Rush Creek: a battlespace adjusted to surprise

Both archaeological and historic sources make it seem that surprise was the basic feature of the Rush Creek fight. The fight was thrust on both sides. Neither was acting with a clear plan, certain information, or definite mission.

Archaeological evidence reveals the fighting at Rush Creek was less intense, and far less threatening than the historic record would lead us to believe (Fig. 9.5). Collins and his men, without question, were surrounded and threatened by many

Fig. 9.5 The number of 12-pdr case shot fragments found at Rush Creek suggests at least one round was fired at the warriors gathering along the old terrace of the North Platte River (authors' image)

hundreds of Cheyenne and Lakota warriors. The archaeological record supports the Cheyenne accounts that, after they crossed to the south side of the river, they took position on high hills well away from the soldiers. That action would be consistent with an attempt to hold the soldiers in their defensive position long enough for the warriors' families to reach safety beyond the temporary position they had near the white bluffs on the north side of the North Platte.

The soldier accounts suggest that the warriors attempted to over-run the position only to be thrown back in desperate fighting. The archaeological record confirms the soldiers' accounts of firing their weapons, Wesson carbines, Spencer rifles, and a few other guns, but what is also clear from the archaeological record is that firing was done at long ranges and the small number of incoming bullets from the Indian firearms found in the entrenchment area suggest the gun fire was not as intense as the soldiers' recollections and reports suggest rather it was, at best, desultory.

The soldiers' accounts, most written 50 or more years after the fight, recalled corralling the wagons end to end to create a defensive perimeter. At least one soldier recalled constructing rifle pits under the wagons, which afforded them greater protection. Collins's official after-action report, written within days of the actual events, states that the rifle pits were placed on small hillocks that provided shelter to the soldiers and created a wide defensive perimeter around the camp. The archaeological record provides ample evidence of the location of the army fighting positions. If 5–10 wagons were corralled in an arc with the wagon boxes touching then they would range from something over 50 ft to over 100 ft in length (15–30 m). An army wagon box was 10 ft (3.04 m) long per regulation. The distance between the low sand dunes where the fired army cartridges were found is over 400 m. This gives Collins's account more credence and suggests a failure of memory in the 50 years after the fact story telling found in the various issues of the *National Tribune*.

One of the most documented events was the charge at the warriors who were within 200 yds (*c.* 180 m) of the entrenchments and under cover of an embankment. This event can be archaeologically documented by lead bullets found to the west of the soldier positions, and by the artillery shell burst artifact distribution, as well as the canister ball. This may well have been the area of the most intense fighting, but the total number of casualties was two soldiers killed in the charge, and perhaps one warrior wounded. There is no archaeological evidence to support Lt Col. Collins's statement that some artillery rounds failed to burst or perform as intended. The archaeological evidence shows that one round of canister was fired, and minimally one round of case shot, at the warriors who had the audacity to get close to the soldier position. If the warriors were within 200 yds/180 m as reported, then the artillery rounds overshot their targets by at least 100 yds/30.5 m. It seems more likely the distance was underestimated or at least overstated, perhaps to engender the feeling that Collins's command was more threatened by swarming warriors that was the actual situation.

The archaeological data is far more in concert with Collins's after-action report and the Bent compilation of the Native American accounts than with the later enlisted men's recollections. There is, however, no question Rush Creek was a site of conflict between the army and Indians on 8–9 February 1865, but the archaeological record shows the later recollections of some of the soldiers is exaggerated in terms of the intensity of the Indian response to the Army presence at Rush Creek.

When fighting started at Rush Creek, the Army forces arranged on local terrain that offered cover and a relatively broad view. The fact that the soldiers described the low raises where Spencer and Wesson cartridges were found as "hills" and "ridges" suggests that they may have been rather substantial elements in what would we are calling the Army's "battlespace". The distribution of archaeological evidence indicates that the Army maintained a clear perimeter, probably near the area that was densely packed with horses, wagons and equipment. We could find no clear evidence of the "breastwork" or other entrenchments that the soldiers supposedly built, but those kinds of investments would have certainly helped the soldier defined and operate in the area they found themselves occupying. They would, in any case, be unlikely to survive in the sandy soil. Even Lt Patton's dramatic cavalry charge may have served primarily to secure the Army's position. It did dislodge a few warriors who were coming close to the Army perimeter, but it was a rather unusual tactic that had tragic results. It also did not resolve the fight. At best it solidified the position the Army held until the Indian forces moved on.

In his after-action report, Collins states that fighting at Rush Creek took place on 8 February and that only minor skirmishing continued during the next morning until noon. When fighting ceased Collins briefly weighed the possibility of crossing the North Platte to continue fighting the Indians, but that plan was rejected. Instead, he decided to keep his command on the trail and to return units to their home bases. At 2 pm on the 9 February he led his command about 15 miles (24 km) up the Platte River toward Fort Mitchell. But even if he had not pursued his adversaries, he remained sensitive to military threats. The next morning Collins split up his command. To assure that there were adequate forces at Fort Laramie, Lt Brown was dispatched with a detachment of the Ohio cavalrymen to protect that critical base. Collins himself took the wagon and a large part of his command back to Mud Springs to pick up the troops left there. After that, he moved along the trail, determining the condition of post and the telegraph systems. As he surveyed this strategic terrain, Collins proceeded with caution. When his scouts spied distant activity, he formed a defensive posture until it became apparent that the party they had met were men of the 7th IVC who had come up from the Julesburg repairing telegraph lines. By 14 February Collins was back at Fort Laramie setting down his account of the North Platte campaign (Collins Report, OR).

When fighting at Rush Creek ended, the Cheyenne community moved in a different direction. Continuing as they had planned into the Sand Hills, the

Cheyenne and their allies looped around to the northwest. They retained their combative posture and met other communities who shared their anger. By the summer of 1865, the Cheyenne community that had fought at Rush Creek was part of large fighting force that emerged on the North Platte valley in Wyoming and engaged U.S. forces in several pitched battles. At one of these, near the Platte River Bridge on 26 July, 1865, Lt Col. Collins's son Caspar was killed.

At Rush Creek, Cheyenne and Lakota warriors were suddenly presented with a battle that was far different from what had been happening just days earlier in Mud Springs. At Rush Creek, conditions dictated that they fight a rear guard action, minimizing their exposure and risk by nearly surrounding the soldiers, but taking positions on the high ground from 200 to 600 yds (180–550 m) and perhaps up to 1000 yd (900 m+) from the army positions. The warriors apparently sought to tie down the Army column so that their families could get safely away from the North Platte River valley and the menace of Collins's soldiers. The Cheyenne and Lakota were entirely successful in this endeavor, leaving them with a tactical and strategic victory over the volunteer cavalry at Rush Creek.

10

Fighting on the North Platte as military operations

Investigation of the battlefields of the North Platte Campaign of 1865 began as a straightforward undertaking in conflict archaeology. As events of the Civil War era, it was reasonable to expect that systematic metal detection and other techniques of battlefield research would work well with these sites. And as is often the case with historical archaeological, a good deal of documentary information was available on this combat. The opposing sides and their motives were known. The context of the conflict and the causes of the fighting had been discussed. The arms involved in the fighting were familiar and the dates and timeline of the combat were documented. The exact location of the Rush Creek fight was initially not known, but discovering that spot seemed like a reasonable challenge. When the bullets and cartridges of the Rush Creek encounter were discovered we were pleased, but not surprised. We knew they were there, someplace.

As the project proceeded, a couple of developments that were essentially incidental to archaeology presented themselves and moved the research past consideration of specific combat points and towards investigation of spatial dimensions of conflict. First, as field research was underway, the application of LiDAR mapping spread across Nebraska and up the North Platte River. This resource, which was entirely new and innovative when it appeared, allowed for detailed topographic assessment of archaeological materials and the terrain on which it was present, regardless of vegetation cover. The second factor that encouraged geographic consideration of the campaign was the easily managed historical, archaeological, and GIS-based large scale terrain analysis that made it clear that the North Platte Campaign involved more than the two engagements. These techniques, which have become well-established as tools in archaeological remote sensing and spatial recording, made it apparent that movement across space and between combat points had to have been an important part of the North Platte warfare. Movement between engagements and preparations for combat were critical to the both sides. They took time and thought and had to contribute to the fighting that took place at the specific battle sites.

Tools for discovering geospatial information created a need for a conceptual means of considering the spatial side of the North Platte Campaign. Landscape archaeologists offered a way of addressing that topic, but given its combative nature, concepts developed by military theoreticians to describe military activities seemed especially applicable to this research. The North Platte Campaign involved movement across the space, changing tactical situations, and conflict between culturally different forces. Given all of this, the obvious challenge for investigation of the material residues of the 1865 fighting was in explaining how archaeology can offer new information, better understandings, and stronger explanations for the events of the Campaign at the specific level, and in the larger context of conflicted landscapes.

The landscape of conflict

The opening the North Platte Campaign illustrates the utility of the conceptual models we developed and applied in earlier chapters. In broad terms the fighting along the North Platte was a result of tensions that became unmanageable as a consequence of events that occurred both east and west of the North Platte valley. The Sioux War of 1862, that began in Minnesota, forced disaffected Dakota communities farther on to the Plains. The Sand Creek massacre of 1864, in eastern Colorado, presented another mitigating factor for the Cheyenne and other tribes of the Western Plains tribes. Hostility and distress created by these actions led some Cheyenne and allied communities to decide that their situation demanded active war. These broad developments certainly help to understand why warfare developed in 1865, but they do not explain why fighting broke out at the small isolated telegraph station of Mud Springs nor at the low crest the soldiers called Rush Creek. Answers to those questions can be found when the battles are viewed in conceptual terms of battlespace.

After a series of successful raids on ranches and small posts on the South Platte, the Cheyenne who had decided on war were well armed, amply equipped and on their way toward secure isolation in the Sand Hills. As the community moved north they stopped at a camp site in the bluffs of the North Platte valley. From that temporary home base, outriders and scouts appear to have determined that the Mud Springs telegraph station was a convenient target. It was a few miles away from their camp and easily recognized as an attractive target. Closely surrounded by a couple of hills, the Station was poorly defended and easily attacked. The terrain was favorable to the attackers, minimizing exposure to counter-fire from the defenders. The herds of horses corralled at the station were protected by a small party huddled in a single building. Victory was likely, booty was probable, and the terrain would make valorous display easy. This was a positive battlespace for the Cheyenne.

The small contingent of cavalrymen based at the Mud Springs may have been only barely aware of the Sand Creek atrocity and fighting along the South Platte but they were not isolated. They were located on an active leg of the overland trail network and connected to colleagues and the nation via telegraph. They were a small detachment but part of a network arranged to keep the trail open. Their mission was to maintain the flow of traffic and information. Defense of the station itself was secondary at best. Support and assistance was available so, to be successful, all they had to do was communicate their situation and hold out until help arrived.

Mud Springs was not an easily defended location. GIS-based terrain analysis makes it clear that the attackers enjoyed the operational and tactical advantage. The Cheyenne warriors approached the station almost unnoticed. They were able to deploy behind "military crests" of hills, small swales, and below the edge of the terrace on which the station sat. Thus the warriors had the tactical advantage of the terrain and controlled most of the immediate surroundings. The soldiers had only two advantages as defenders: the buildings and the telegraph. The telegraph, before it was cut by the warriors, gave the station defenders the opportunity to alert their superiors and summon help. Although strategically and tactically poorly located, the station's log building provided a solid defensive position that was nearly immune to small arms fire.

As reinforcements from Fort Mitchell and Fort Laramie began to arrive, less than 36 hours after the defenders' message was sent, personnel mass shifted from the favor of the warriors to the soldiers. With combatant numbers nearly even, mounted and dismounted charges by Collins's troops shifted the balance of power. Terrain was no longer a real advantage. Capture of the horses and mules from the corral at the station became difficult and valorous displays were very dangerous undertakings. When the Army established a strategically located rifle pit on the hill south of the station it became nearly impossible for attackers to reach their objective undetected. It is easy to see why the Cheyenne broke off the engagement and prepared to move to safer ground.

Locating cartridges, casings, and other battle debris that marked the Rush Creek battlefield was the major discovery of this project. The quantities were not great but in keeping with the findings from other investigated battlefields (see Chapter 9) and showed where the historically known fighting had actually occurred. This discovery gave the battle geographic reality. It also opened investigation of why the fight occurred where it did and how the landscape had influenced the fighting. After finding the Indian's abandoned camp, the cavalry column understood that they were following the fresh and well-marked trail left by the Cheyenne community. When the column crossed some low knolls about 6 miles (*c.* 10 km) south of the camp, that were the high point on their route, the two sides became aware of one another. Neither side seems to have been doing all the reconnaissance they should have. GIS-based terrain analysis seems to demonstrate that the two forces became aware of one another at nearly the same time. Cheyenne warriors, acting as a rear guard for a community on the move, attacked the point that the cavalry column became visible to the Indian community camped just across the North Platte.

The cavalry discovered their situation when Indian fighters, who had seen them, began an attack. The spot where the fighting occurred seems not to have been planned or selected by either side. It truly was an unexpected and situational battlespace that both sides had to accommodate.

The distribution of archaeological materials on the Rush Creek battlefield is generally consistent with accounts left by the participants. Clusters of expended cartridge cases from the cavalry carbines shows that fighting took place along a circular perimeter. Indian positions were not as easy to discover. This pattern is consistent with historic accounts that describe sudden charges and attacks by individuals and small war groups. The best archaeological evidence for where Indian forces were positioned comes from the remains of two specific cavalry actions recorded at Rush Creek. These comprised a round or two of artillery fire and a mounted cavalry charge. Both of these actions were discovered archaeologically. Remains of both the strap sheet iron of a sabotted spherical shell and a scatter of exploded shell fragments indicated the cannon was located on the western side of the perimeter and shot toward the west. This same area also had a couple of .36 pistol bullets suggesting this area was also the scene of a dramatic cavalry charge. Together, the evidence of artillery and cavalry charge suggest that Indian fighters used the slight bank on the northwest side of the battlefield for cover. They seem not to have occupied any specific areas as firing posts.

Considering the relics and debris of the fights that happened in 1865 at Mud Springs and Rush Creek in light of modern military concepts seems to offer insights into why the combat developed as it did. This research helps us understand the actions of the men who fought these battles. We hope it will also illustrate the power and appropriateness of conceptual consideration of conflict sites. These two fights were, however, rather minor affairs. A few men were killed and others could count it as important experience or worthy service. But can these battles help us understand broader aspects of Western History?

Battlespace requires a context, a place, essentially terrain on which to move combatant and support elements. Battlespace in modern warfare, along with military terrain analysis, is a means to inform commanders, at various levels, of what they may be facing, how best to maneuver across a field of battle to best exploit their combat strength, and to minimize risk to their troops.

Archaeological and historical analysis of battles essentially reverses the process by using terrain analysis to understand how battles played out on the landscape, how troops moved across the ground, employed cover, and to discover avenues of approach that may no longer exist or are disguised by modern development. This type of terrain analysis provides researchers and land managers with information on how to interpret the past, assess the effect of modern intrusions on the historic landscape, and determine appropriate preservation measures or even the value or significance of a historic battlefield.

Even the most unexpected and apparently randomly located engagement involving substantial numbers of combatants requires immediate tactical decisions and some attempt at an organized response. The Mud Springs and Rush Creek fights present different archaeological appearances. The differences between the battles should not, perhaps, be surprising. As a complex phenomenon, combat can be expected to involve different responses and deployments depending on the specific situation. Native American and Union combatants had diverse military skills based on their culture and training, but all had the ability to adjust and innovate. Still, expecting diversity does not *explain* the observed variation seen in disparate battles. Viewing the archaeological differences apparent at these battles in terms of the strategic, operational, and tactical issues exposed by the Levels of War and battlespace models offers a context for assessing the differences of the battle records. It offers a means of linking the material evidence of battle to higher levels of war.

Lt Col. Collins responded to a specific threat, the attack on Mud Springs, when he was informed by telegraph. His situational awareness was largely dictated by his mission of guarding the overland trail and protecting communication lines. He may not have had the numbers of troops to be actively aggressive and seek out the Cheyenne and their allies who were raiding civilian and military ranches and stations along the trail. Perhaps that was not his mission or, at least, how he interpreted his mission. In any case Collins's leadership style was reactive rather than proactive. He responded immediately to the threat posed at Mud Springs with a strong force of cavalry and artillery – the forces he had available. Once he had reduced that threat he followed the warriors' trail in order to find and subdue the raiders, or at least to recapture stock and supplies looted from trail ranches and Julesburg.

If Collins's leadership style was reactionary then the Cheyenne leadership was far more aggressive. The Cheyenne had a war-time model imbedded in their cultural view of the world. After the Sand Creek massacre they went into conflict mode in a dramatic and effective manner. Attacks along the trail were intense. Whether the attacks were designed to replace supplies lost at Sand Creek or simply revenge is not an easy question to resolve. Both were clear motivating factors. Within the warrior culture of the Cheyenne, coming together in time of crisis was not new. Aside from achieving the goals of resupply or vengeance it offered warriors, especially young men, the opportunity to gain status by valorous display and action against their enemy – an aspect of native cultural behavior that may, in hindsight, seem foolhardy to modern eyes but which represented a crucial rite of passage for the young warriors seeking to establish their place in society.

The Cheyenne took advantage of the landscape in which they resided in an effective and efficient manner. They moved across wide-ranging expanses of the Plains, keeping U.S. forces off-balance. The war leaders were effective at making the army forces react to the Cheyenne aggressive posture. The army may have held the ground at Mud Springs and Rush Creek at the end of those fights, but they were really Cheyenne victories from a strategic and tactically view.

The fighting in the Platte River valley of Nebraska may have ceased in mid-February 1865, but the conflict with the Cheyenne, Lakota, and other Native American groups was only beginning. It would continue with various levels of intensity until 1877, and arguably until 1890. Though not as a result of Mud Springs, Rush Creek, or the Platte River Bridge fights, which nevertheless certainly influenced military thinking at higher commands, the Army began a much more aggressive campaign to subdue these groups over the next year or so. That campaign failed and it was only with the return of regular troops to the trans-Mississippi West after the Civil War that the balance of power shifted to the U.S. and the era that we perceive as the Indian Wars began.

In 1865 Indian and army forces were strategically very different, but neither side seems to have aimed at total destruction of the other. Native communities sought security, materials and war honors, while the mission of the Frontier Army was occupation and protection of transportation and communication routes. Combat with neighboring societies was a standard part of life for Native communities of the Plains. And it was not until 1869 that Phil Sheridan made his famous – and usually misquoted – assessment, "The only good Indians I ever saw were dead." (Morris, 1992, 342–3).

In this work we have endeavored to demonstrate that while all of the terrain based analyses noted are valuable they are often site specific. Applying the concept of battlespace allows for a broader understanding of spatially separated but temporally linked events. It not only allows us to better interpret site specific events, such as the Rush Creek fight, but it allows us to see the larger context of the events that led to Rush Creek, specifically the fight at Mud Springs. Battlespace provides us the framework to employ and engage the high-powered analytical tools in computer based GIS programs. The advent of LiDAR imagery has dramatically improved our capability to see and explain landscape use by employing the analytical power of GIS and the theoretical model of battlespace as a means to further our understanding of how different groups and different cultures used the landscape over which they roamed.

Battles and skirmishes in the trans-Mississippi West during the Civil War, such as Mud Springs and Rush Creek, were usually smaller and of shorter duration than most battles and engagements east of the Mississippi. Likewise, there were fewer cases of later fighting on the same or nearby ground. This has resulted in most Civil War and other battle sites in the trans-Mississippi area being single-use or single occupation sites, making the archaeological record far easier to discover, analyze, and interpret than the battlefields and camps east of the Mississippi. Drier climatic conditions and far less modern industrial and residential development in the western half of the nation also allows for better preservation of the conflict sites in the West. Those sites, given the potential for good preservation of physical evidence, their smaller size, and singular nature, provide an ideal testing ground for applying models of conflict archaeology, especially the battlespace model.

Battlespace appears to hold significant promise as a broad-ranging middle-range theoretical model to test in other archaeological warfare and conflict sites. The model should work well with sites that have historic documentation and well-preserved archaeological evidence of conflict. The model is eminently suited to the study of historic conflict, even at the low level and small scale of the North Platte Campaign.

Appendix 1: transcriptions of enlisted men's accounts of the fights

1. E. M. Drake: *National Tribune*, 28 November 1889

E. M. Drake, Co. B, 11th Ohio Cav., Red Oak, O., writes that he has never seen an account of the Rush Creek fight with Indians, which occurred at Mud Springs Feb. 5, 1865. The writer was one of the advance scouts. Wm. O. Collins, Colonel of the 11th Ohio Cav., with about 100 of the regiment, including some of the 7th Iowa Cav., was attacked by an overwhelming number of Sioux. From early in the morning until evening the battle raged, and finally the Indians withdrew. As they did not renew the fight on the next day, and as the soldiers had been reinforced by 50 men and one 12-pounder gun, it was decided to pursue the Indians. After a march of 10 miles the troops came to the deserted camp of the enemy on Rush Creek, and the trail was followed down the Creek to the North Platte, which was then frozen over. On the opposite side the Indians were seen pouring out from the hills, and they appeared to outnumber the troops ten to one. The Colonel set his men to digging trenches, and when the Indians came within range the boys sent a shell into their midst, which created quite a commotion. All day long they were kept away by constant firing, but about 4 the next morning the savages charged the breastworks, and a hand-to-hand fight followed. After much desperate fighting the Sioux fell back; but the writer feels sure that, if it had not been for the good management of Col. Collins that day, not one of the command would have been alive to tell the tale. As the troops were eating breakfast on the morning of the following day the Indians charged once more, but again were beaten off, and the troops were enabled to march back to Mud Springs.

2. George Rowan: *National Tribune*, 30 January 1890

Fighting the Sioux

Correcting the Statement of an 11th Ohio Cavalryman

Editor National Tribune: In a recent issue of your paper I see an article headed "Fighting the Sioux," in which E. M. Drake, Co. B, 11th Ohio Cav., states "that he has never seen an account of the Rush Creek fight with the Indians, which occurred at Mud Springs Feb. 5, 1865." Mr. Drake then submits his version of the fight, with dates and numbers, much of which is inaccurate, and his first and greatest error is that the Rush Creek fight should have occurred at Mud Springs, for they are different places, separated by about 10 or 15 miles, and were separate battles fought on different days by the same parties.

Again, it is a fact that this same band of Indians burned the Town of Julesburg, on the South Platte, fought and killed about 22 of Co. F, 7th Iowa Cav., and that fight occurred on Feb. 22, 1865. This news was wired Col. Collins, of the 11th Ohio Cav., then at Fort Laramie, before the Indians resumed their journey northward, for immediately thereafter they left the South Platte, via Pole Creek, stripping the telegraph poles of the wire as they came, and to their astonishment met at Mud Springs Col. Collins, with parts of Cos. B and D, of the 7th Iowa Cav., and a small squad of his own regiment, at which time the fight at Mud Springs above referred to took place, which could not have been earlier in the month than the 25th of February.

Mr. Drake states that "Wm. O. Collins, Colonel of the 11th Ohio Cav., with about 100 of the regiment, including some of the 7th Iowa Cav., was attacked by an overwhelming number of Sioux." That is erroneous, for there was a mere Corporal's guard of the 11th Ohio in the Mud Springs fight, and the artillerymen, who did not arrive until after the battle, did not number more than 25 men, while Cos. B and D, of the 7th Iowa, mustered about 120 men. True the battle at Mud Springs lasted one day, and after reinforcement of the 25 of the 11th Ohio, with a little 12-pound gun, the Colonel decided to pursue the Indians. Therefore, on the morning of the second day we followed their trail northeast to the North Platte where the waters of Rush Creek empty into that river, and the stream being frozen over, the Colonel's orders were to march on to meet the Indians, who by this time were coming out of the hills on the opposite side of the river in great numbers, which we estimated at 50 to our one, and who would have met us on the ice where the greatest victory the Indians ever won, and the greatest slaughter that ever occurred in the West would have taken place (the Custer massacre not excepted) had not nearly all the commissioned officers of the command earnestly advised the Colonel to fall back to a commanding position on the banks of Rush Creek, where the two days' siege took place, known as the Rush Creek fight, to which Mr. Drake refers.

After taking our position on the banks of the creek, throwing up works was an easy matter as the soil was very sandy and easily removed; hence, by the time the battle commenced the breastworks were fairly under way. Much of the credit is due to the Lieutenant of the 11th Ohio Cav. For the able manner in which he handled the little gun, which no doubt saved the lives of us all. That the Indians charged our breastworks once or twice, and a hand to hand fight followed is erroneous; and more especially is it an error that they charged at 4 o'clock in the morning, for at that season of the year it was dark at 4 o'clock in the morning, and Indian depredations are most invariably committed in daytime. In fact, the only charge made was by the soldiers, who charged to dislodge Indians, who had crept so close to our breastworks that they were pouring volleys of lead and arrows into our lines, and the honor of leading this charge belongs to the above mentioned Lieutenant of the 11th Ohio: but he was followed by boys of the 7th Iowa almost exclusively.

Our commanding position, the manipulation of the small gun, and the above mentioned charge, is what saved our lives, none of which was the good management of Col. Collins, for the position we took was urged upon the Colonel, and the Lieutenant was instructed to handle the gun to the best of his ability, which he did, and the same Lieutenant who led the charge went to the Colonel an asked permission to make the charge, which was granted; and again it is a well known fact that we did not return to Mud Springs, but marched direct to Fort Laramie.

Although Col. Collins was a good man, yet as a soldier and an officer he was a mere cipher with shoulder-straps. Twenty-five years is a long time to remember dates and numbers, consequently Comrade Drake is excusable for his errors.

I think my impartial statement, though perhaps not absolutely correct, yet more accurate and impartial than Mr. Drake's, because he barely mentions the 7th Iowa Cav., and scoops the honors for Col. Collins and the 11th Ohio Cav., both of whom cut the smallest figure in the fight, and, worst of all, wholly ignores the brave Lieutenant of his own regiment, above referred to, and whose name, I am sorry to say I have forgotten. George W. Rowan, Co. D. 7th Iowa Cav., Chehalis, Wash.

3. George Nelson: *National Tribune*, 1 May 1890

OUT ON THE PLAINS.

The Mud Springs and Rush Creek Affairs.

Editor, National Tribune: By way of correcting E. M. Drake's statements in the issue of Nov. 28, and also Geo. W. Rowan's account in the issue of Jan. 30, I propose, if you will allow me a small space in The National Tribune, to write a correct account of the Mud Springs and Rush Creek fights, which I feel the more competent to do from the fact that I kept a diary from March 7, 1861, to March 7, 1865, and which, in the form of a small passbook, is on the table before me as I write.

Feb. 4, 1865, the commander of the Post at Fort Laramie received a dispatch from Mud Springs, 110 miles distant, to the effect that the station was surrounded by a large number of Indians, and that unless speedily succored the 14 men at that place (five civilians and nine soldiers) would be killed or captured. Col. Collins, of the 11th Ohio Cav., realizing the importance of prompt action, started about dark same day to the rescue.

The command consisted of parts of four companies of the 11th Ohio Cav., about 100 men, and Co. D, 7th Iowa Cav., about 50 men, in all about 150 men, well mounted and armed in most part with Spencer rifles and carbines. It will be seen by the above that the 11th Ohio Cav. furnished a pretty strong "Corporal's guard."

We marched all the night of the 4th and until about 11 o'clock of the 5th, when we arrived at Fort Mitchell, one-half the distance to Mud Springs. Here we rested and refreshed ourselves and horses until about 7 p.m. when we resumed our march, the Iowa company under Capt. Foutz [*sic*] having been sent on in advance. Marching all the night of the 5th we arrived at Mud Springs about 7 o'clock on the morning of the 6th, which is the date of the Mud Springs fight, and not the 5th, as stated by Comrade Drake, nor as late as the 25th, as stated by Comrade Rowan. Meantime the 11 men in the station, which consisted of two small log houses used for telegraph office and stable, reinforced by the Iowa company, who by the way were splendid fighters, had made it so hot for Mr. "Lo" that they had made but little headway toward reducing the station. Having marched for two nights and a day in terribly cold weather, with no sleep and but little rest, we were in rather a sorry plight, many of the men having their hands and feet badly frozen.

We were in no condition to resist the assaults of overwhelming numbers, yet we did so successfully. The number of Indians was estimated at 1,500 to 2,000. Hastily forming a corral out of our few wagons, and thus securing our stock, we prepared to give them a warm reception, and they came at us in fine Indian fashion. Soon after the fight began Col. Collins telegraphed to Laramie for reinforcements. The "affair" continued without intermission from 7 a.m. till dark. Our loss was very light compared with that of the Indians, as we did most of our fighting from the two log houses mentioned, while they were in the open. The Indians made several desperate attempts during the day to stampede our horses and mules and get them out of the corral. Many of their "braves" bit the dust, or rather the sand, in these attempts, and brought them within close range of our unerring Spencers. We could not ascertain with any degree of accuracy how many warriors were killed, as most of them were tied to their ponies, a custom they have to prevent their killed from falling into the hands of their enemies. The fight ended at dark by the Indians drawing off. We rested on our arms during that night and the day of the 7th, not, however, relaxing our vigilance. Never was a day of rest more welcome to poor mortals than this 7th day of February, 1865, was to us. During the night of the 7th, the reinforcement, consisting of 60 of the 11th Ohio, with cannon, arrived.

We now had about 180 or 190 men able for duty, having lost 20 to 30 men killed, wounded and frozen since leaving Laramie. With this small force Col. Collins concluded to pursue and "catch" the Indians. Catching them was an easy enough matter, but we had a terribly hard time letting them go, as the sequel will show. Following their trail, which they made no attempt to conceal, we came up with them on the 8th, about 15 miles from Mud Springs. When we arrived at the Platte, opposite the mouth of Rush Creek, we could see the Indians in great numbers on the opposite side of the Platte, which was frozen over solid, so that we could have crossed easily. This Col. Collins wanted to do, and attack them in the hills. I quite agree with Comrade Rowan that had this been attempted, the result would have been similar to the Custer massacre on the Big Horn, in June, 1876.

Better councils prevailed, however, and it was determined that if they would fight they should do so on ground of our own choosing. As soon as they saw we were not going to cross the river, they came pouring out of the bluffs by the hundreds, the ice on the river being literally black with them. It was now that we did the most effective work with our cannon, as we got in several very good shots while they were in a compact body on the ice. We only got in a few effective shots, however, as they scattered out into small squads, but they kept coming all the same till all of them were across. Meantime we had been busy preparing to receive them. We had a very strong position made by digging a trench in the sand, and throwing up the sand thus removed for a breastwork, as described by Comrade Rowan. The Indians now had us surrounded, except on the side next the Platte, and it seemed as though the prairie was literally alive with them. True, we had a very strong position, but they outnumbered us at least 10 to one; were well armed, well mounted, cunning and brave; in fact, they fought like old warriors from away back. About 200 to 300 yards from our ditch was what seemed to be a long, low place, or dry branch, where the grass and sage brush had grown very rank, and the dead grass having fallen down, afforded good concealment for the redskins. Two of them would get on a pony, and riding swiftly through this place, one of them would slip off. This they kept up until this place, which commanded our position, was literally filled with warriors, and they picked off our men at every opportunity. Our situation was growing more desperate every minute. But the redemption of that ravine was close at hand.

Lieut. Patton, of the 11th Ohio, asked permission to take 20 picked men and charge into the infernal nest and rout the Indians out. This was not readily agreed to, as it was a desperate and dangerous undertaking, and we had no men to spare. But something must be done, and it was finally granted, and Lieut. Patton, forming his men in "line" and giving a few parting and final instructions, gave the command "forward," and into the "nest" they went pell-mell and out the Indians went – those of them who were not killed or wounded. The 20 men, after emptying the two revolvers that each carried, started to regain the breastworks. The Indians now rose up from all sides and in the middle, to try and cut off the gallant Lieutenant and his little band. This, however, we had expected and from our breastwork we fired into them a most murderous volley, that made them recoil, and gave the charging squad a chance to get back. Two men were killed in the charge, – Harris, of the 7th Iowa, and Billy Hartshorn, of the 11th Ohio. The chargers were principally 11th Ohio men, of the old battalion as we called them, who had been on the frontier more than three years and were good Indian fighters. Comrade Rowan, therefore, is in error in saying that the Lieutenant was followed in the charge "almost exclusively by Iowa troops." This charge and the volley from our position virtually ended the fight, the Indians recrossing the river and disappearing among the hills on the opposite side of the Platte. The next day we started on our return to Fort Laramie, getting back on the 11th. I do not wish to be understood by this as imputing to anyone a disposition to make a misstatement willfully; far be it from me to do that, but I fear Comrade Rowan has got the Julesburg affair, where Iowa troops suffered so severely (Feb. 22), and the Mud Springs and Rush Creek affairs slightly mixed. We used to speak of it as the "Rush Creek fight," when speaking of the two fights, which is probably what Comrade Drake meant by the Rush Creek fight fought at Mud Springs, etc. But he is mistaken in regard to the Indians charging us at 4 in the morning; either that or I was sleeping so soundly that I heard nothing of it.

I am not certain as to the name of the Lieutenant who led the charge, but think it was "Bob" Patton; if incorrect, hope some comrade will correct me. – Geo. W. Nelson, Co. I, 11th Ohio Cav., Eaton, O.

4. David C. Peck: The *National Tribune,* 10 March 1898

IN THE INDIAN COUNTRY.

A Brief Campaign That Was Full of Fighting.

Editor National Tribune: Our company (H, 11th Ohio Cav.) built Fort Mitchell, and while stationed there we received telegraphic notice that a small outpost called Mud Springs had been attacked by the savages, and asked for help.

This was about 4 o'clock p.m. "Boots and saddles" was sounded by the buglers, and every man who could be spared was soon in the saddle, and on the way to Mud Springs. The post was situated at the foot of small bluffs on one side and a small valley on the other.

We arrived about 2 o'clock a.m.; the company halted and the bugler was ordered to sound the bugle, so that the besieged would know that help was at hand. There were only seven soldiers and four citizens to guard and protect the post.

When we got to the boys the doors were thrown open and an old soldier named Idlet cried for joy. The boys knew that it was the intention of the Indians to crawl up around the building in the night, and if a head appeared it would be sure death.

At daylight 16 of us (I among the number) were sent to the bluff in the rear of the post to prevent, if possible, the Indians from getting too close. We had fired several rounds at the Indians as they had galloped from one bluff to another, when about five hundred rose up behind the creek bank and fired at us. As the fire was too heavy to withstand, the order to retire was given, and just as we turned to go two brothers, one standing on each side of me, were shot. I was the last one to get into the building. One of the men, who had been shot through the shoulder, soon came to and ran as fast as his legs could carry him, and I opened the door. He stepped in, fell, was picked up, placed in a bunk and given medical attention.

The other brother had been shot in the hip, the ball lodging in his groin. We could see the Indians jumping up, waving their scalping knives and yelling like demons.

There was a sunken place in the ground where he lay, and he had presence of mind enough to roll himself over into that and draw his revolver, which he intended to use on the first Indian who showed himself after that.

As bullets and arrows were coming against the building like hail, William Hall, who had seen service in the frontier and after being discharged had enlisted again in my company, asked if there was any one who would volunteer to go with him and bring in the wounded man. No one would go; he took off his revolver belt and hung it on a peg, as unconcerned as though he was going to his supper. Officers tried to persuade him not to go, as it was almost sure death, but he opened the door, walked quickly out to the man, and placing him on his shoulder brought him safely into the house without getting even a scratch. I think the hand of Providence was surely manifested there.

The brother wounded in the shoulder got well, but the other comrade we laid under a mound on the plains.

We fought the Indians there two days, when they left, and we followed them to the Platte River, near Brush [Rush] Creek, where we fought them two days more. They then retreated over the mountains.

In the meantime we had been reinforced by the 7th Iowa and one piece of artillery. When we reached the river, which was frozen over, and got into position, the redskins had started to re-cross the river. There were several hundred on the ice. The cannon was double-shotted and let loose on them. A swatch was cut through them, but it did not check them, and a few solid shot were fired which had the desired result for awhile.

Soon afterwards about three hundred then got into a hollow a few hundred yards from our corral and were wounding our boys so fast that 29 volunteers were called for and soon responded, and put under command of Lieut. Geo. W. Marsh. He told them that no one was to retreat until ordered to do so.

Among the number was a comrade by the name of Hartshorn, whose horse would run away every chance he got. He was asked not to ride the horse, but he would do it. A charge was made, and for a while you could not tell soldier from Indian. True to his nature, Hartshorn's horse ran away. The Indians opened up a way and let him through. He commenced to hit his horse by the side of the head, thinking thus to turn him towards camp. The Indians closed in on him and that was the last seen of the poor fellow until next day, when a few Indians (the main body having by this time gone over the mountains) were seen standing on a bluff, about a quarter of a mile away, apparently interested in some object.

A gunner was ordered to double-shot the cannon, and see if he could displace them. He fired, and in a moment there was not an Indian in sight. The gun was reloaded, and about twenty of us went up to where the Indians had been seen.

There lay poor Hartshorn with his head crushed in, one arm off at shoulder, one hand off, both legs off at the knee, his breast cut open and his heart gone, in his body were 97 arrows. His body was placed in a wagon, taken to Fort Mitchell and given burial.

We had been there two days and nights with nothing but hardtack and raw flesh to eat, as we were not allowed to build fires. When we started for the fort, the mule teams were put into a gallop and no time was lost in getting shelter and something to eat.

Boys, give us your recollections of old Sitting Bull, Little Thunder, our old guide Bridger, etc. David C. Peck, Co. H, 11th Ohio Cav., Rush Run, O.

5. Eli S. Ricker interview with A. G. Shaw, Co. B, 11th OVC (Jensen 2005)

Before he interviewed Shaw, Ricker made the following note.
Valentine. A.G. Shaw. Has photos of Spotted Tail and his assassin Crow Dog, White Thunder & Two Strike, & Sioux history in hieroglyphics from the year 1000 to 1872; & he was on Little Bighorn battleground next day after battle. Came to the west as a soldier in 1862 in 11th Ohio Cavalry & is full of Hist. Mr. Craven says he is reliable. Can tell about Fort Casper. Knows the whys and wherefores of the wars and Agency troubles.

Interview with A. G. Shaw, of Valentine, Neb., Sunday, Sept. 1. 1907. (this line crossed out in original)

... Another incident in the history of the 11th Ohio Cavalry was the battle the Reg't. had with the Indians at Rush Creek on the Platte above Ash Hollow 18 or 20 miles. The Reg't. went first to Mud Springs (then in Idaho territory, now in Neb., he says) which is east of Courthouse Rock, on the trail from [Lodge] Pole Creek to the Platte, just before and in sight of the Platte. This was in January, 1865. Mud Springs had been a stage station but was now abandoned as such & was at this time a telegraph station. There were several buildings, and rooms connected or a part of the same building. The Indians got behind the hill in the rear of the buildings & would crawl to the top and shoot down into the log building. There were no windows on that side, but occasionally a bullet went through the chinking and penetrated to the inside, but nobody was hurt. The attack was begun at daybreak and kept up with irregular intervals of suspension until sundown. Ceased altogether then. The Cmdg. officer sent soldiers to the top of the hill to reconnoiter the enemy's position, and several were wounded, one belonging to Co. B. fatally.

Next morning the command moved down on the trail to Rush Creek & went into camp on a low bluff overlooking the river on the south side; and the wagons were corralled by bringing the fore wheels up to the hind wheels of the wagon in front till the boxes of the two wagons met, except on the north side of the camp next the river. This was in January [February], 1865.

On the north of the river the country was open and slightly rolling but not sufficiently so to hide a horse. The camp was formed about noon. There was seen what appeared to be a forest of pine trees in the distance. The Colonel examined with his glass and discovered this appearance to be a dense swarm of Indians coming toward the camp. The soldiers were ordered, notwithstanding the ground was frozen, to dig rifle pits within the enclosure and so the men could shoot under the wagons. Before the preparations were all made the savages began the attack. Shots came into the corral from the surrounding hills. Indians came up ravines and got within fifty yards of the camp. The colonel was the first one shot; he was struck by a spent ball on his shin bone. The Colonel asked for volunteers to charge this ravine and drive out the Indians. Charge was made & Inds. dislodged. One soldier was carried by his unmanageable horse in among the Indians and next day his body was found filled with arrows. This was the only casualty among the soldiers. The Inds. escaped across the river on the ice. The mountain howitzer was turned on them and this sunk some Inds. horses and riders through the ice. This occurred about evening and the Indians disappeared. The command hitched up and moved back to Fort Laramie.

Appendix 2: sites open to the public

Scotts Bluff National Monument

190276 Old Oregon Trail, Gering, NE 69341

Towering 800 ft above the North Platte River, Scotts Bluff has served as a landmark for peoples from Native Americans to emigrants on the Oregon, California and Mormon Trails to modern travelers. Extending over 3000 acres the park contains many interesting geological formations and historical sites, including that of Fort Mitchell, though there are few traces of the fort today. There is a visitor center, and many miles of bike/hiking trails. There are living history events throughout the summer months.

Trails are open every day, sunrise to sunset, except Thanksgiving, 25 December, and New Year's Day. There is a small charge per vehicle for entry.

Oregon Trail Museum and Visitor Center opening: Summer Season (June–August): 8 am–7 pm; Winter Season (September–May): 8 am–5 pm. Summit Road closes 30 minutes before the visitor center.
Website: https://www.nps.gov/scbl

Chimney Rock

PO Box F, Bayard, NE 69334-0680

Designated the Chimney Rock National Historic Site, Chimney Rock is one of the most famous and recognizable landmarks for pioneer travelers on the Oregon, California, and Mormon Trails, located on the south edge of the North Platte River Valley. The Chimney Rock Visitor Center is located 1.5 miles south of Highway 92 on Chimney Rock Road. It houses museum exhibits, media presentations, and other educational materials concerning life on the overland trails, and a museum shop.

Opening hours: The Visitor's Center is open 9 am to 5 pm daily including Memorial Day, 4 July and Labor Day but is closed on State holidays. There is a small admission fee.
Website: http://www.nebraskahistory.org/sites/rock/

Legacy of the Plains Museum

2930 Old Oregon Trail, Gering, NE 6934
This new museum is still under development in 2016. Located on the Oregon Trail, it features an impressive collection of pioneer and early community artifacts, antique tractors, and farm implements; an 80-acre working farm; historic farmstead structures; living history events and striking views of Scotts Bluff National Monument.
Opening hours: Summer (1 May–31 Oct.): Monday–Saturday: 9 am–5 pm; Sunday: 1–5 pm; Winter (1 Nov.–30 Apr.): Monday–Friday, 9 am–4 pm, or by appointment.
Website: http://legacyoftheplains.org/

California Hill

Upper Crossing of the South Platte River – Brule, Nebraska: Highway 30, about 4.5 miles west of Brule
The crossing of the South Platte River on the Oregon Trail at California Hill was the most important because it led directly to Ash Hollow, the best approach to the North Platte River. California Hill presented a climb of 240 ft in just over 1½ miles in order to reach the plateau between the North and South Platte Rivers. Imposing trail ruts are still plainly visible most of the way up the hill. There are spectacular panoramic views back toward California Crossing.
Website: https://www.nps.gov/oreg/planyourvisit/site5.htm

Ash Hollow State Historical Park

PO Box A, Lewellen, NE 69147
Ash Hollow lies on the California National Historic Trail just south of Lewellen (U.S. Hwy 26). After negotiating the climb up California Hill, travelers on the main overland trail crossed the high tableland between the South and North Platte rivers before descending Windlass Hill into the North Platte Valley through Ash Hollow. Wagons descended the 25° slope of Windlass Hill for about 300 ft and trail ruts can still be seen on the ground surface.
Website: visit: https://www.nps.gov/cali/planyourvisit/site1.htm

Courthouse and Jailhouse Rocks

About 6 miles south of Bridgeport on State Route 88
Courthouse and nearby Jailhouse Rocks lie just south of the Oregon National Historic Trail and were the first of several impressive natural landmarks along the trail in western Nebraska.
Website: https://www.nps.gov/oreg/planyourvisit/site6.htm

Fort Kearny State Historical Park

1020 V Road, Kearney, NE 68847
Fort Kearny was established by the U.S. Army in 1848 to protect the growing traffic along the Oregon Trail from the threat of Indian attacks. It was strategically located at a junction where various trails merged to follow the Platte River 330 miles west to Fort Laramie. None of the original structures survive but the stockade, parade ground, and blacksmith's shop have been reconstructed as part of a small interpretation center and the park is open daily for hiking, biking, and camping.
Website: https://www.nps.gov/oreg/planyourvisit/site4.htm

Fort McPherson National Cemetery

12004 South Spur 56A, Maxwell, NE 69151
Built in 1863, Fort McPherson (formerly Fort Cottonwood) was established at a strategic location near the Platte River to ensure peace along the western frontier between the immigrants traveling along the Oregon Trail and the Native American inhabitants. The troops originally stationed at the post provided military protection from hostile Native Americans during the construction of the railroad. In 1873, a national cemetery was established at the site of the fort. The initial purpose of the cemetery was to provide an appropriate burial ground for remains of soldiers that were brought from remote, abandoned posts on the western frontier. Significant interments include 63 African American Buffalo soldiers from the 9th and 10th U.S. Cavalry who served in the West during the Indian Wars. The fort itself is no longer visible.

The cemetery is open daily from dawn to dusk.
Website: http://www.cem.va.gov/cems/nchp/ftmcpherson.asp

Nebraska History Museum

131 Centennial Mall North Lincoln, Nebraska 68508
Recently refurbished and reopened, exhibitions cover 12,000 years of Nebraska history.
Opening hours are 9 am–4.30 pm, Monday-Friday; 1 pm-4.30 pm, Saturday and Sunday
There is a voluntary entry fee.
Website: www.nebraskahistory.org/sites/mnh/

Fort Laramie National Historic Site (Wyoming)

965 Gray Rocks Road, Fort Laramie, WY 82212
Situated on a bend in the Laramie river close to its confluence with the North

Platte, Fort Laramie was developed out of a buffalo trading post into one of the principal military posts on the Oregon Trail. Eleven structures of the fort are now restored and refurbished to their historic appearances and the remains of other buildings can also be visited. There are living history events throughout the summer months.

The park Museum and Visitor Center is open daily except Thanksgiving, Christmas, and New Year's Day 8 am–4.30 pm, with extended hours Memorial Day–Labor Day: 9 am–7 pm. The park grounds are open daily sunrise to sunset. Entry is free.
Website: https://www.nps.gov/fola

Sand Creek Massacre National Historic Site (Colorado)

910 Wansted POB 249, Eads, CO 81036

Site of the massacre of at least 180 Cheyenne and their allies, mostly women and children, by the U.S. Army on 29 November 1864. Although there is little to see on the ground the site was designated a National Historic Site in November 2000 to "recognize the national significance of the massacre in American history, and its ongoing significance to the Cheyenne and Arapaho people and the descendants of the massacre victims." There is an active Interpretive program offered daily or by appointment.

Opening hours: open all year 9 am–4 pm, closed on weekends 1 Dec–31 March and on Thanksgiving Day, Christmas Day, and New Year's Day. Entry is free.
Website: https://www.nps.gov/sand/index.htm

Bibliography

Ashmore, W. and Knapp, A. B. (1999) *Archaeologies of Landscape: contemporary perspectives.* Blackwell, Oxford.

Babits, L. E. (2013) METT-T, KOCOA, and the principles of war: a template guiding a better understanding of battlefield behavior and detritus. In *From these Honored Dead: Historical Archaeology of the American Civil War*, eds C. R. Geier, D. D. Scott, and L. E. Babits, 262–270. University Press of Flordia, Tallahassee FL.

Barnes, J. (2008) *Forts of the Northern Plains: guide to the historic military posts of the Plains Indians Wars.* Stackpole, Mechanicburg PA.

Beck, P. N. (2013) *Columns of Vengeance: Soldiers, Sioux, and the Punitive Expeditions of 1863–1864.* University of Oklahoma Press, Norman OK.

Bell, T. and Lock, G. (2000) Topographic and cultural influences on walking the Ridgeway in later prehistoric times. In *Beyond the Map, Archaeology and Spatial Technologies*, ed. G. Lock, 85–100. NATO Science Series, Series A: Life Sciences 321, IOS Press, Amsterdam.

Bleed, P. and Scott, D. D. (2008) *The Mud Springs Fight: Archeological Evidence and Diverse Records of a Frontier Battle.* Department of Anthropology and Geography, University of Nebraska-Lincoln, Lincoln NE.

Bleed, P. and Scott, D. D. (2009) Archeological interpretation of the frontier battle at Mud Springs, Nebraska. *Great Plains Research* 19 (1), 13–26.

Bleed, P., De Vore, S. L., Scott, D., Renner, A. and Young, A. (2014) Archeological *Investigations of Overland Trails and Civil War Era Features at Mud Springs Station and the Rush Creek Trail Crossing in Western Nebraska.* Midwest Archeological Center, National Park Service, Lincoln NE.

Burton, R. F. (1963) *The Look of the West, 1860; Across the Plains to California.* University of Nebraska Press, Lincoln NE.

Caporaso, A. L., Carlson-Drexler, C. G. and Masters, J. (2007) Metallurgical analysis of shell and case shot artillery from the Civil War battles of Pea Ridge and Wilson's Creek. *Technical Briefs in Historical Archaeology* 3, 15–24. (http://www.sha.org/publications/technical_briefs/volume03/article03.cfm).

Collins, W. O. (1886) *Official Records of the War of the Rebellion, Ser. I 48 Pt I.* Government Printing Office, Washington DC

Connor, M. and Scott, D. D. (1998) Metal detector use in archaeology: an introduction. *Historical Archaeology* 32 (4), 73–82.

Department of Defense (2015) *Department of Defense Dictionary of Military and Associated Terms, 8 November 2010 (As Amended Through 15 June 2015)*, JP 1-02. http://www.dtic.mil/doctrine/dod_dictionary

Diffendal, R. F. (1993) Understanding ground water starts with the rocks: geologic framework, groundwater occurrence and irrigation development in Nebraska. In *Flat Water: A History of Nebraska and its Water*, eds R. D. Kuzelka, C. A. Flowerday, R. N. Manley, B. C. Rundquist, and S. J. Herrin, 50–54, Resources Report 12, Conservation and Survey Division, Institute of Agriculture and Natural Resources, University of Nebraska-Lincoln NE.

Dyer, F. H. (1994) *A Compendium of the War of the Rebellion, Volume II.* Broadfoot Publishing, Dayton, OH (1st edn 1908).

Espenshade, C. T. (2014) Landscape of battle: military terrain analysis of the Battle of Credit Island. In *Archaeology of the War of 1812*, eds M. T. Lucas and J. M. Schablitsky, 229–51. Left Coast Press. Walnut Creek CA.

Foard, G. and Curry, A. (2014) *Bosworth 1485: a battlefield rediscovered*. Oxbow Books, Oxford.

Greene, J. A. and Scott, D. D. (2004) *Finding Sand Creek: history and archeology of the 1864 massacre*. University of Oklahoma Press, Norman OK.

Griffith, P. (1986) *Battle in the Civil War: generalship and tactics in America, 1861-1865*. Field Books, Camberley.

Griffith, P. (1989) *Battle Tactics of the Civil War*. Yale University Press, New Haven CO.

Grinnell, G. B. (1910) Coup and scalp among the Plains Indians. *American Anthropologist* 12, 296–310.

Grinnell, G. B. (1956) *The Fighting Cheyennes*. University of Oklahoma Press, Norman OK (revised from 1915 edn).

Gunther, J. Di. and Gunther, C. O. (1935) *The Identification of Firearms*. Wiley, London.

Haack, S. (2007) From Sand Creek to the Powder River: George Bent's year of warfare as related in his letters. Manuscript copy in possession of Peter Bleed.

Haag, L. C. (2006) *Shooting Incident Reconstruction*. Elsevier, Boston MA.

Halaas, D. F. and Masich, A. E. (2004) *Halfbreed: The Remarkable True Story of George Bent - Caught Between the Worlds of the Indian and the White Man*. De Capo Press, Cambridge MA.

Harris, C. E. (1980) Sherlock Holmes would be impressed. *American Rifleman* 128 (5), 36–39, 82.

Hart, H. M. (1967) *Pioneer Forts of the West*. Superior Publishing, Seattle WA.

Hatcher, J. S. (1943) *Textbook of Firearms Investigation, Identification, and Evidence together with Textbook of Pistols and Revolvers*. Small-Arms Technical Publishing, Plantersville South Carolina SC.

Hatcher, J., Jury, F. J. and Weller, J. (1977) *Firearms Investigation, Identification and Evidence*. Stackpole Books, Harrisburg PA.

Heard, B. J. (1997) *Handbook of Firearms and Ballistics*. Wiley, New York.

Henderson, P. (1951) The Story of Mud Springs. *Nebraska History* 32 (3), 108–19

Hewett, J. (ed.) (1997) *Supplement to the Official Records of the Union and Confederate Armies, Part II, Record of Events 50, Serial No. 62*. Broadfoot Publishing, Wilmington NC.

Hoig, S. (1961) *The Sand Creek Massacre*. University of Oklahoma Press, Norman OK.

Hyde, G. E. (1968) *Life and Times of George Bent: Written from His Letters*. University of Oklahoma Press, Norman OK.

Jensen, R. E. (ed.) (2005) *The Settler and Soldier Interviews of Eli S. Ricker, 1903-1919*. University of Nebraska Press, Lincoln NE.

Jones, E. E. (2006) Using viewshed analysis to explore settlement choice: a case study of the Onondaga Iroquois. *American Antiquity* 71 (33), 523–38.

Jones, R. H. (2005) *Guarding the Overland Trails: The Eleventh Ohio Cavalry in the Civil War*. Arthur C. Clark, Norman OK.

Keeley, L. H. (1996). *War Before Civilization*. Oxford University Press, Oxford.

Llobera, M. (2007). Reconstructing visual landscapes. *World Archaeology* 39 (1), 51–69.

Mattes, M. J. (1969) *The Great Platte River Road: the covered wagon mainline via Fort Kearny to Fort Laramie*. University of Nebraska Press, Lincoln NE.

McChristian, D. (2009) *Fort Laramie: military bastion of the High Plains*. A. H. Clark, Norman OK.

McDermott, J. D. (2003) *Circle of Fire: the Indian War of 1865*. Stackpole, Mechanicburg PA.

Mcfeaters, A. P. (2008) Frontier artillerists and the gun that shoots twice: interpreting artillerist behavior at Alkali Station, Nebraska. M.A. thesis, Dept of Anthropology, University of Nebraska-Lincoln.

McKee, W. R. and Mason, M. E. Jr (1995) *Civil War Projectiles II Small Arms and Field Artillery*. Publisher's Press, Orange VA.

McNutt, R. K. (2014) Finding forgotten fields: a theoretical and methodological framework for historic landscape reconstruction and predictive modelling of battlefield locations in Scotland, 1296–1650. PhD dissertation, Centre for Battlefield Archaeology, School of Humanities, University of Glasgow.

Melton, J. W. Jr. and Pawl, L. E. (1994) *Introduction to Field Artillery Ordnance, 1861-1865.* Kennesaw Mountain Press, Kennesaw GA.

Morris, R., Jr. (1992) *The Life and Wars of General Phil Sheridan.* Crown Publishing, New York.

Otterbein, K. F. (2004). *How War Began*, Texas A&M Press, College Station TX.

Robrock, D. P. (1983) The Eleventh Ohio Volunteer Cavalry on the Central Plains, 1862–1866. *Arizona and the West* 25 (1). 23–48.

Scott, D. D. (1994) A sharp little affair: the archeology of the Big Hole Battlefield. *Reprints in Anthropology 45.* J and L Reprints, Lincoln NE.

Scott, D. D. and Mcfeaters, A. J. (2011) The archaeology of historic battlefields: a history and theoretical development in conflict archaeology. *Journal of Archaeological Research* 19 (1), 103–34.

Scott, D. D., Bleed, P. and Bilgri, B. (2011) Archaeological investigations of the 1865 Rush Creek Battlefield, 25MO81, Morrill County, Nebraska. *Central Plains Archeology* 13 (1), 79–129.

Scott, D. D., Fox, R. A. Jr, Connor, M. A. and Harmon, D. (1989) *Archaeological Perspectives On the Battle of the Little Bighorn.* University of Oklahoma Press, Norman OK.

Secoy, F. R. (1992) *Changing Military Patterns of the Great Plains Indians.* University of Nebraska Press, Lincoln NE.

Smith, M. W. (1937) The war complex of the Plains Indians. *Proceedings of the American Philosophical Society* 78 (3), 425–61.

Steinacher, T. L. (1995) NESHPO and NRCS archeological remote sensing survey at Fort Robinson, Scottsbluff, and Mud Springs, Nebraska. MS report on file, Nebraska State Historical Society, Lincoln NE.

Swinehart, J. B. and Diffendal, R. F. Jr (1995) *Geologic Map of Morrill County, Nebraska.* Miscellaneous Investigations Series, U.S. Geological Survey, Washington DC.

Swinehart, J. B., Souders, V. L., Degraw, H. M. and Diffendal, R. F. Jr (1985) *Cenozoic Paleogeography of Western Nebraska.* Rocky Mountain Paleogeography Symposium 3 eds R. M. Flores and S. S. Kaplan, Rocky Mountain Section, Society of Economic Paleontologists and Mineralogists, Denver CO.

Tipping, R., Cook, G., Mauquoy, D., Bersfored, A., Hamilton, D., Harrison, J. G., Jordan, J., Ledger, P., Morrison, S., Paterson, D., Russell, N. and Smith, D. (2014) Reconstructing battles and battlefields: scientific solutions to historical problems at Bannonckburn, Scotland. *Landscapes* 15 (2), 119–31.

Turney-High, H. H. (1991) *Primitive War: its practices and concepts.* University of South Carolina Press, Columbia SC.

U. S. Army (1986) *FM 7-70 Light Infantry Platoon/Squad.* Department of the Army, Washington DC.

U. S. Army (2001) *FM 3-0 Operations.* Department of the Army, Washington DC.

U. S. War Department (1851) *Instructions for Mountain Artillery*, Gideon, Washington DC.

Ware, E. F. 1(994) *The Indian War of 1864.* University of Nebraska Press, Lincoln NE (reprint of 1906 edn).

Weber, K. P. and Scott, D. D. (2006) Uncapped potential: applying firearms identification procedures in the analysis of percussion caps. *Historical Archaeology* 40 (3),131–43.

Wheatley, D. and Gillings, M. (2002) *Spatial Technology and Archaeology: the archaeological applications of GIS.* Taylor and Francis, New York.

Index

Numbers in italics denote pages with images